THE REVENGE OF
INDIAN PETER

THE REVENGE OF INDIAN PETER

The Incredible Story of Peter Williamson

Rosemary Linnell

Book Guild Publishing
Sussex, England

FT

First published in Great Britain in 2006 by
The Book Guild Ltd
25 High Street
Lewes, Sussex
BN7 2LU

Typesetting in Garamond by
Keyboard Services, Luton, Bedfordshire

Printed in Great Britain by
Antony Rowe Ltd, Chippenham, Wiltshire

A catalogue record for this book is available from
The British Library

ISBN 1 85776 949 X

To
Heather and Ian Gilbert
who first told me about Peter Williamson
and gave invaluable help and advice
during my researches

Foreword

Rosemary first heard the story of Peter Williamson's extraordinary life from the daughter of the minister of the parish where Williamson was born. Her research took her to Edinburgh where she was able to consult the two books that Williamson wrote about his adventures and the depositions and reports of the various lawsuits he brought which are in the Advocates' Library, also in Edinburgh.

Williamson had such a dramatic early life that Rosemary felt that it would be better to tell his story in narrative form rather than a straight-forward biography. However strange it may seem, this accout of Williamson's life is true and only in one or two cases where there is no record of someone's name has she had to invent one for them.

David Linnell
August 2005

Chapter 1

'Too many children and dogs,' James Maclaurin muttered as he went dot-and-carry, dot-and-carry through the Edinburgh wynds. They should be indoors in such wet weather, he thought, not getting under an old man's feet!

He stabbed his cane at yet another sodden urchin and hobbled on towards the law-courts. The water ran from his three-cornered hat and sluiced in the channels of the cobbled street. What could have possessed young Andrew Crosbie to send him out on such a day as this? After all, he was no longer a lawyer's clerk, not since he had left to nurse his poor sick wife all those months ago. And since she had died no-one had ordered him about, least of all a young whipper-snapper of a grey lawyer whom he had carried on his shoulder and made a pet of ever since the lad was old enough to walk. Oh, he had been glad enough of the copying Andrew or his father had given him to do, but this was different; this was wet, cold and highly suspicious.

Maclaurin was glad that it was getting dark. He did not want anyone that he knew to see him ducking through the entrance to the law-court where the little shops called the Luckenbooths stood all crowded together. Most of the places were empty, the day's trading being over, but from one door there was light and the sound of murmuring voices. Outside hung a board with 'Peter Williamson, late of the New World' painted on it and against the closed shutters a chalked notice asking people to walk in.

The chairs and tables had all been cleared from the eating house and everyone was forced to sit on the floor. Maclaurin hung his cloak and hat on a peg and found himself a space in the corner. There were already quite a few important-looking men in the room. They seemed content to sit fatly around the space, their legs spread out in front and their backs against the walls which were, like the floor, not

1

over clean. He noticed very few women and wondered whether it was simply idle curiosity that had drawn all these folk there on such a wet evening.

After a while the doors were closed and the room became dark. In the centre of the space, a hearthstone had been set out and a small fire of pine wood and sweet grass whispered and purred gently on it. The smoke was not unpleasant but the walls of the room soon became lost, so that one did not seem to be in a building, but in some shelter outdoors. He could hear owls and other strange birds that whooped and mourned in the dark. Everyone in the room hushed at the strangeness of it, and then the drumming began. The sound seemed to be all round, and yet it was soft and the rhythm strange and quick. Then the voices ... maybe one voice, maybe more. Maclaurin had heard the gipsies and tinkers when they came into town singing in high, lamenting voices, but this singing had no words, only thin, cut-off sounds, breathy and with a dying rasp in the throat. Strange and sad sounds repeated over and over in the dark, with only the drums, soft and rhythmical, underneath.

'Hey gah, hey gah, hey gah, ney hey.'

Someone must have come into the room at this time, for there was a breath of movement at the fire and then a taper thrust into the flame and resin torches passed around to light the room. Now the man was clearly visible but still no word was said by anyone. He was sitting on a heap of spruce boughs by the fire, wrapped in a blanket; all alone in the centre of the room and smoking a pipe of tobacco. It was a strange, long pipe with a red clay bowl shaped like an axe, with feathers hanging below. After a while he drew deep on it, breathed out a smoking sigh, laid the pipe aside and spoke.

He was not naked as Maclaurin had heard, but fully dressed with feathers on his head, his dark hair untied and hanging snakily about his ears, his face painted with red earth and with white stripes between the eyes and on his cheeks. He threw off the blanket that covered his shoulders and spoke of the clothes he wore and how the skins of deer are worked soft and supple to make the breeches, boots and shirt. Beads, porcupine quills and shells decorated the sash, belt and pouch that he wore. About his neck hung a powder-horn and a metal crescent on a chain.

2

The voice went on, telling in simple words how he had lived with the Delaware Indians and learned their ways. There was nothing to explain how he came to be a captive, only that he had been for nine months their prisoner and travelled with them, so that he had come to know their ways, to understand and speak some of their language and to experience their ferocious cruelty.

Everyone in the room sat so still it seemed the man was alone with the pictures he was creating. There was a strange grandeur in his description of Indian savagery. No-one in that group of bewigged, eighteenth-century gentlemen, their waistcoats strained across their ample stomachs and sitting, clumsy and ridiculous, on the floor, could fail to be moved by the things he told. Oh, they could read in books and listen to the fables told by sailors but here was a genuine painted Delaware who could take them straight into the forests and mountains of the New World. Much of his story was of terrible suffering but they could perfectly believe that a young warrior was called a brave, and that to bear pain and torture was a test of honour. They were carried away by the story and it seemed perfectly proper that any man, if he were to cry or faint or struggle, would be accounted less than human, and that this man, this Peter Williamson, was such an Indian 'brave'. Who did not believe, as if they had felt and seen for themselves, that he had endured without cry or tears, torture and burning, nakedness and hunger, long marches and humiliation ... a captive in a strange land.

As Williamson spoke, he slowly took off his finery, unlaced his moccasins and, wearing only a fringed loincloth and with the scars of his torture clearly evident on his body, took a bundle of sticks upon his shoulders. They were looped about with a flat, woven braid that crossed his forehead like the harness of an ox and so, bent under the weight, he shambled barefoot and in silence from the room. Instead of a proud warrior, inhabitant of the wilderness, they were left with the image of a shuffling bond-slave.

Someone cleared his throat. There was a slight shifting of position, but no-one dared look towards his neighbour. Men and women of reason and learning had sat, like children at the nurse's knee and heard stories that made them weep and be afraid, and now they were ashamed to be seen. They had been other people in another world and now they had to come back again into themselves.

A woman, wispy and pale, came through the inner door, admitting light and draughts that carried the stale smoke into the corners of the room. She had an old collecting box which like an elder of the kirk she thrust under the noses of the congregation.

'I hope you liked the show, sir. Did you enjoy it? He only does it to raise funds. Thank you, sir. It is very tiring to him, and doing it sometimes brings him bad dreams and then we're both kept from sleep.'

Maclaurin stuffed a handful of small silver through the slotted lid she held out to him and hastily thrust his way into the fresh air. He felt drugged and sick, but whether from the herbs on the fire or from the strangeness of the spell the man had cast, he did not know.

Strangely disturbed he hobbled homewards. What was the man playing at? Everyone knew that Red-Indians were cruel savages, but Williamson had turned their cruelty into heroism. Everyone knew that they were heathen brutes, but he had shown that they worshipped God in every thing that was made. What right had he to go against common belief, to deceive everyone with his sweet smoke and outlandish noises? The man was a conjurer, a common deceiver, and it was long past time to be safe at home away from mourning shadows and dark, haunted forests.

*

The next day was bright and clean, and the wind brought the smell of fields and the promise of summer into the Edinburgh streets. Maclaurin made his report to the two Crosbies, father and son, sitting in the visitor's chair in the front office. He felt uncomfortable, as though he was a hostile witness and the two lawyers were about to tear his evidence apart. The older man – Alexander Crosbie – was a creased, frowning giant who was never seen without his dark gown and the starched Geneva bands that stood out below his furrowed chin. Although he visited the barber regularly there were bristles of grey hair in the folds of his skin, that no razor seemed able to reach, and which had earned him the nickname of 'Boar-hunt Crosbie'. Andrew, his son was a pale young man with light grey eyes and wisps of pale hair that hung softly under his grey lawyer's wig. He was writing notes, folded up in the clerk's chair, where Maclaurin had often sat when he worked for them and where he would have preferred to be on this bright morning.

The two men heard his story out. Maclaurin had tried to be as factual as possible, but all the time the strange, high singing ... 'hey gah, hey gah, hey gah, ney hey' ... rung in his head and he could not get rid of the scarred, shuffling figure of Indian Peter that stumbled through the dark space behind his eyes. It angered him that he had been so moved by a mere performance. He was stale and flat from lack of sleep, for he had dreamt of dark forests and being hunted by something he could not see and, once having started awake, he had sat up by his window until dawn.

'You know he wants us to take his case?' The senior Crosbie's voice was loud enough to bring him back to the present.

'Aye, sir, I do.'

'And you know that he charges wrongful arrest and theft against the authorities in Aberdeen?'

'Aye, sir, I do that!'

'And now that you've beheld the man, what do you think of him?'

'I'm no longer your clerk, Mister Crosbie. You must do as you think fit.'

'But we asked you to go and sound him out because we wanted your opinion. Now do as you would have done when you were my clerk. Would you advise us to take his case?'

Maclaurin could hold his peace no longer. He jumped out of the hated chair and turned on the two lawyers. 'The man's a charlatan, a mountebank, a gaol-bird and probably a liar! That show of his ... it's magic and mumbo-jumbo, made to work evil dreams and fantasies. He was arrested dancing like that and exhibiting himself in war-paint and savage nakedness in the streets of Aberdeen, and the book which they tore up and publicly burned was some lurid account of his adventures. The man is not to be trusted, sir, and if you take him on you will be the laughing-stock of the country!'

'Well, that's clear enough at any rate! But it's not me that will take his case, James. It's my son here who will go down in history as the man who defended Peter Williamson.'

Maclaurin was breathless after his outburst and sat down again.

Why had they asked his opinion if they had already decided to take the case? Go down in history he would, the young fool, as the idiot of the law-courts! This was the lad he had loved like his own son, to whom he had taught everything he knew! Why must he be so obstinate?

Andrew looked up from his notes and said quietly, 'I have but one question to ask you, James. What was in the pages that were torn out and burnt?'

Maclaurin stared at Andrew. 'He says that they described how he was kidnapped off the streets of Aberdeen and sold into slavery in America!'

*

Through the summer of 1760 and well into the autumn James Maclaurin stayed quietly at home, copying the sheaves of law papers that were sent round by a stream of small child-messengers. Then one day the footsteps that climbed to his rooms were not the light tread of children, and when he opened the door it was Andrew who stood outside.

James was not pleased. He fussed and squawked about like a broody hen, pushing piles of unwashed clothes into corners and brushing crumbs off the one decent chair in the place. 'You might have warned me,' he grumbled. 'I've been busy – all thanks to you, of course – but I've had no time to clean and polish...'

'James, James! I did not come here to inspect your living arrangements. I came because last time you grumbled at me for fetching you out in the rain. Sit down and let me tell you my news. Is that pigeon trying to get in?'

The pigeon was a daily visitor to the clerk's window which was so high that even the trees would have been below. Not that there were many trees in that part of the city. James put a scrap or two of bread on the window-sill to satisfy the bird and the two men settled down to talk.

'What brings you this way, Mister Andrew?' said James, pummelling a cushion and offering it to his guest.

'We would like you to gather some more evidence on the Williamson case.'

'You've decided to take it then?'

'Indeed, yes, and you are not to scold me. We have been to the Lord Ordinary, Lord Minto, and he accepts that there is a case to answer, but, as I said, we need your help. We have everything we can get from "Indian Peter" himself but, as you well know, James, we cannot bring a charge against person or persons unknown. We need names.'

'Names? Whose names? What sort of names?'

'The names of those responsible for arresting him.'

'And where will I find those names? Always supposing I agree to look.'

'You'll have to go to Aberdeen for that I'm afraid.'

'Now hold on, sir, just hold on! You want me to go to Aberdeen? At my time of life? Is there no person of your acquaintance in that city who could do it? Can the man himself not go ferreting for you, without me going all that way and winter coming on?'

'James Maclaurin! I never thought you one to shirk his duty! Who better than yourself to accompany Williamson, and make sure he does not get himself put into the tollbooth again?'

'Accompany Williamson! Go along with that mountebank showman? Why I'd never dare to show my face again if I'd run off with a travelling circus!'

'Just be still and listen! When you saw Indian Peter was it not something more than a fairground side-show? Admit it! You were deeply affected by it. And, besides, he would never dare to repeat the performance this time round ... not with you to keep charge of him. We've the Edinburgh Court's permission to get witnesses, signed and sealed, and as a further safeguard, should you need it, you'll not travel by road. A passage has been booked for you on a trading vessel out of Leith, in the name of Jamieson, father and son.'

'So I'm to be father to the man now am I? You were very sure of me it seems! Andrew, I'm older than your father by a week or two. We've worked together, he and I, all these years. I would willingly be your father in any venture, but this fellow... Why should I go, that mislikes the man so thoroughly? Why send anyone when he has papers that he can show and knows exactly what to look for?'

'It's just because you have such a healthy distaste for the business that we want you to go – to sort out the truth from the pretence.

You can take depositions; you can report back just as you did after the show; you know the law better than most. You are our right arm in this business; who could we trust better than you?'

Maclaurin knew when he was beaten and before long all the details for the journey were fixed. Andrew's young cousin, Moira, a girl of sixteen and convent bred, was given the task of fitting him out with plaid and bonnet, two pairs of warm mittens and stout new shoes. She even found him an old bag to put his things in, so that he looked like a crofter come out of the hills, and felt like a fish out of water.

Chapter 2

Williamson met him on the quayside. It was a damp morning with a sea-mist and only a pale, white disc of a sun to see them off. Maclaurin was ill at ease, not being much used to the sea, but Williamson took him over with a twinkle in his eye, and all the authority of a regular sea-faring man.

'Come away, father. I'll put your wee baggie below, and we'll be gone with the tide.'

Maclaurin winced at his tone but followed him obediently into the cramped cabin-space that had recently been used for carrying wine, judging by the smell of wood and brandy that still lingered there. There were bunk beds that Peter claimed were the height of luxury but looked to James like cat-boxes, and a table screwed to the floor. No chairs, no place to store anything except a hook on the wall and a small sliding panel under the bed.

'We should sleep soundly tonight with this smell as a night-cap, and with the wind as it is we should be there in a day or two. You take that bunk, Father, and I'll stretch out here.'

'Do you have to call me father? There's nobody by to hear.'

'Oh, I think I should, don't you? It'll come easier in future if we're well rehearsed in our rôles. I'll not presume on the title any further than the duty owed his father by a dutiful son, but it gives you the right to beat me if you feel the need!'

Maclaurin could think of no answer to that, so they went on deck and watched the grey bank of the firth slip further and further into the mist as they headed into the shipping channel and made towards the North Sea.

*

He had no idea how wretchedly ill he would feel the moment they

9

cleared the coastline. The ship was a fat little lady, built for the Baltic trade, and bound for Rostock after picking up goods in Aberdeen. No doubt she rode the waves as smoothly as her captain and Peter assured him she did. But James Maclaurin was no sailor and he took immediately to his berth and swore to remain there.

'You'd feel better for the wind in your face and some food in your stomach,' Peter said, cheerfully grinning at his wan face and painful moaning. 'Come on, man, you'll soon find your sea-legs and begin to enjoy yersel'.'

'How long do we have to put up with this?'

'We'll be about five days, the skipper says. She's not built for speed is the *Lady Grace*, but she'll do us fine.'

Peter's determined cheerfulness was yet another grievance in Maclaurin's mind. He had not wanted to come in the first place; he was too old and set in his ways to undertake adventures lightly and he disliked his companion more than ever. The suspicion he had of Peter Williamson had not grown less but had intensified as time went by. He found his cheerful voice and bluff manners hard to tolerate in the close quarters of the tiny cabin and when Peter came in, as he did every hour or so to see how he fared, he turned to the wall, more to be rid of him than through the sickness.

*

When morning came, after that first gloomy day and night, Maclaurin was surprised to find that he had slept. Peter woke him with a cup of thin, barley gruel and a piece of oatcake, and stood over him while he supped at least some of it; then he took the old man completely by surprise by sweeping him up, blanket and all, and carrying him up onto the deck. Williamson was not a big man but he had an undue strength in him and seemed to make nothing at all of loading Maclaurin onto his shoulder and humping him around like a sack, treatment which did nothing for the old fellow's self respect or for his temper.

'Put me down, you great gowk! Are you mad? You'll have me overboard. Put me down!' Which Peter did, in a sheltered nest that he'd arranged for him among piles of cordage on the deck.

'There y'are, Fayther,' said he, grinning as wide as a turnip lantern.

10

'You'll do fine there. I've carried heavier than you, many a time. I've taken loads of fur and hides on my back and carried them through rushing water and over rocks. I've taken a canoe out of the water and piled that over my head beyond white water rapids for mile after mile. So what makes you think I'd drop my own dear father into the salt sea, just when I'm about to make his acquaintance for the first time!'

Maclaurin grunted and eased himself into the tarry heap, but he was not so displeased, at that. He and Margaret had had no children ... no grandchildren, and no little nephews or nieces either, and now he was finding himself unaccountably drawn to this irrepressible joker who called him father.

'What on earth were you at, carrying furs? Were you working the docks?'

'Na, na. That was after my slave-master died ... before I was captured by the Indians.'

Maclaurin did not understand a word. Peter sat himself down beside him on the rope and drew out a pipe – a small, dirty white, clay pipe this time – and busied himself with filling and tamping the bowl. He said nothing more, no explanation. James tried to sort out what he knew from Peter's story of his journey with the Indians, but what the rest of it meant he had no idea.

'Where was this, then? In America?'

'Aye. I was free for a while, and travelling the land. I carried loads. I worked for many men of all nations and tongues. I lived in the back country, in the woods. I worked the rivers and saw the great falls where the spray rises above the forest like smoke. The Indians say that if a bird flies into the spray, it dies. They pick the bodies out of the water and pluck and eat them: geese sometimes, wild geese that come down from the snows.'

'Who was this man you call the slave master?'

'Mister Wilson. He bought me in the slave market in Philadelphia. The City of Brotherly Love!'

'Then you were a servant! You had indentures. There's a good many men, poor men, who go off to make their fortune in the New World and begin by being indented servants, and none the worse for that!'

'Oh aye, but they go willingly, or hadn't you heard? Mister Wilson

11

was just such a man. He treated me well. I've no complaint there. But I was sold to him against my will. I was taken from my family, from school and from my home and sold against my will. I was only twelve years old!'

'Who did that?'

'I don't know.'

'But you must know. Who sold you? Who got the money?'

'The captain of the ship got the money. The ship was wrecked so he took the money.'

'Now, now, this is going too fast. I cannot keep pace with any of this. I don't know what is true and what is fantasy, and anyway none of it makes sense to me!'

'You're like those douce baillies and magistrates in Aberdeen that arrested me. You don't understand, so you say it cannot be true. Well, it is true. It did happen. And I'm sorry if you don't believe me!'

'Hold on to your bonnet and don't lose patience with me. I am trying to sort out what it is you're telling me and what it is we're going to find when we get to Aberdeen. Andrew says there must be something in your book that makes the authorities there afeared. Something they don't want made public. He thinks they knew that what you said in the book was all true. That you were kidnapped ... trepanned ... as you say. The book is burnt, so I cannot read it for myself, but since we are shut up together in this miserable wooden bucket, why don't you start at the beginning and see if you can make me understand. If I'm forced to work with you I might as well be put in the picture.'

So it was that Peter Williamson told his story, in more detail than ever he put in his book. He had told it many times before, but always dramatically, cutting it to the bone, shaping it to the needs of his audience who were on their way to market, or sitting on the bare floor in the theatre of his room, or on noisy street corners. Never had he had such an audience as this old man, who, grasping at the inexplicable and questioning the detail of every moment as he reached out for understanding, forced Peter to remember things he had forgotten, had not even known he knew, about the story of his childhood days and his growing up.

Chapter 3

There was another autumn day he remembered: the day it had all begun. He sat on the table while his father, his real father, savagely cut his hair. There was no rhythm to it; no pleasure in a job well done. Peter watched the tufts fall to the floor and was puzzled. There seemed to be too much of it, enough to cover two heads. He wondered if there was a way to stick it back on again. The room was so quiet that the sound of the shears seemed unnaturally loud behind his ears, as if he was hearing it through his skull. He turned his eyes as far as he could without moving his head and saw that the whole family was still there, sitting around the walls watching the tufts of hair falling. Not a word – snip, snip, hardly breathing, waiting for the end.

At last his father shook out the towel that had covered his shoulders and lifted him down. Then, carefully shifting the scissors from one hand to the other so that the points were turned towards himself, he made a little bow and handed them back to Aunt Mary.

'There you are, Mary. He's all yours! Humble-headed. Newly shorn like a lamb to the slaughter.'

Peter had seen Aunt Mary arriving in a flurry that morning but she had not seen him. The carter had brought her to the road-end and she had walked the half-mile to Hirnley, stumbling in her city shoes and looking like walking cow-parsley, Peter thought, with her lace cap, apron and shawl among the bushes and long grass. He had not bothered to turn back. Since mother died there had been many visitors, offering advice and help and talking over his head. Besides the Michael Fair at Aboyne began the next day and he was off to watch. Maybe someone would let him help set up the rings for the cattle show, or arrange the trestles for the stalls and sideshows. He might even earn a penny or two running messages. He would stay out the whole day and, with any luck, Aunt Mary would have gone by the time he returned.

He took the path that followed the stream down the hill. Some of the water was turned aside and pounded through a grid into the mill close. He loosened the debris of leaves and sticks that was caught there and the water thanked him, chuckling in newly found freedom, hurling itself onto the huge, backward-turning wheel. The fine spray soaked through his shirt as he stood there, gazing against the sunshine at the perpetual rainbow and listening to the drumming of the water. He was so deafened that at first he did not hear the other drum.

It was a huge drum: brightly coloured, and so large that the red-headed man who was beating it 'peram-peram' with both hands, had to lean back to balance the size of it against his belly. He walked like a blind man that could not see the road in front of him, legs stiff and straight, feeling the way for pitfalls. 'Peram-peram!' He should have been leading a victorious army into Aboyne, instead of the raggedy bunch that were following him: men, and women too, young girls some of them, chattering and marching and looking about. Peter scrambled over the bank into the roadway and fell into step behind them, shadowing a dark, red-lipped man with a whip, who was bringing up the rear.

As they turned into the field where the fair was to be held Peter dodged ahead into all the bustle and to-and-fro of the stallholders. He fetched and carried, held the heads of the heavy cart-horses, pulled, pushed and lifted all through the dusty day until the men were called home to their suppers and the horses were stabled for the night. He had earned nothing, but he had been given apples and a piece of pie and he had seen the fair built up from a stretch of overgrazed pasture into a whole city of enclosures, trestles and booths. The men with the drum and the whip, and all their ragged army had disappeared and it was time for home.

He knew what was waiting for him. Jeannie would tell on him to Father, and Father would get the switch out of the corner and give him a couple of half-hearted strokes across the back of his knees in token punishment. There was no heart in his father these days to beat him, as he used to do, in anger. Father never got angry these days. He never laughed either. Mother had been quick to laugh and invent reasons to stop work and tell stories or play games. Then the pot would boil over or the washing would fall in the mud and Father would be angry and shout because there was nothing but bread and dripping for supper. Jeannie would take charge even then. She would scold Mother and set things to rights, as if Mother were the child and she the wife.

'You're old before your time, Jeannie maidel. Life's too short. Enjoy it while you can,' Mother would say, as if she had known how short her life would be. Now she lay, her dead baby beside her in the churchyard, and Jeannie had taken up her big apron and her responsibilities.

'She's more than a mother to those bairns,' they said, shaking their heads sadly. The pots were scoured and gleaming, the washing aired and folded. The two older boys, Alex and Martin, were given responsibility for feeding the pig and the few moulting hens and tending the vegetable patch. The three little ones, two boys and a girl, grew fat and bonny. Their clothes were clean and mended and they played quietly by themselves on the doorstep, like three sleek mice. Only Peter caused any trouble. Not to be trusted with responsible tasks, not content to play around the house, he was always running off over the fields, to be sought for and brought home in disgrace.

This Michaelmas eve, however, there was no scolding. Auntie Mary was still there, and everyone was on their best behaviour. She was Mother's sister. A widow, she lived in Aberdeen and had always refused to spend a single night under James Williamson's roof. 'This place is a pigsty,' she would say and take her leave abruptly. But now, here she was in Father's chair, and showing no sign of leaving even though the evening shadows grew long outside and the turf burnt down in the grate.

Jeannie put a bowl of oatmeal on the table for Peter, who took off his boots without undoing the laces and sat down at the centre of that silent family circle. Baby food, he thought, now I'm really in disgrace. But there was the remainder of a bramble tart on the table and, when nobody shouted at him for taking a large bite, he finished it up as though he had won a victory.

They were talking over his head again. Auntie Mary was dictating a long list of things to Jeannie – stockings, shirts, a comb... It was then that she demanded he have his hair cut.

'I will not have him coming with me, looking as though he's been dragged through a hedge backwards!'

Before Peter had a chance to sort out the first question from the hundreds that crowded his head, Jeannie had cleared the table and clattered out into the scullery, Aunt Mary had produced scissors from her bag, Alex had found a towel, his father had lifted him onto the table and the snipping began. Peter thought Jeannie had been crying when she crept back in, but that hardly seemed likely, as Jeannie never cried.

Peter listed questions in his head like a school test and then answered them himself. Why was he having his hair cut? Because he was going with his Auntie Mary. Why was he going? Because she had come all this way to fetch him. Where was she going to take him? To Aberdeen, he supposed. That was where she lived.

There seemed only one question left. For how long?

He had never spent a night away from home, but they had mentioned spare shirts and stockings. It would take the best part of a day to get there. Perhaps he would spend the night at her house. He wondered what her house was like and whether he would sleep in a bed. The only time any of them slept in a bed was when they had a fever and lay in Mother and Father's bed during the day. Perhaps he had better not ask how long he was to be away in case he was disappointed about the bed. In the end he asked no questions at all but ran his hand over the prickly stubble of his head and went outside to the privy. While he was down the garden he dug a small hole beside the apple tree and buried the steel buckle that had fallen off Mother's shoe. At first he had kept it to tease her ... afterwards he had kept it as a remembrance.

*

The next day the carrier arrived earlier than expected and there was a rush and a panic to leave. The whole family came down as far as the road to see them off and to help Auntie Mary up beside the driver. Peter sat facing backwards at the tail of the cart, watching his childhood getting smaller and smaller in the distance. They passed dozens of people on the road, out early, making for the fair. Peter had no regrets about missing it. His best day had been yesterday.

16

Yesterday it had been *his* fair; today it belonged to anybody and everybody.

The carrier was telling Auntie Mary all about everybody's fairs. About Michael Fair in Charlestown of Aboyne, about Bartle Fair in Kincardine and Briack Fair in Tarland.

'There's a parcel of folk gaen wi' a piper and a drum proclaiming and inviting persons to gae wi'em to foreign parts.'

At which Auntie Mary clicked her tongue and said that she had heard that some folks were so at their wits' end with the poor living a few years back that one wife had sent her husband to the plantations and some fathers had been forced to send away their sons that were a burden to them.

For some reason they were rather quiet after that and Auntie Mary gave Peter a whole piece of gingerbread.

*

Even facing backwards Peter could tell when they were nearing Aberdeen. The air smelt different, with a new, raw chill in the throat, and there were the gulls. At this time of the year there were hundreds of gulls inland, following the autumn ploughing; but today it seemed as though every screaming bird in the country was here. They hung and swooped and complained in great grey clouds and Auntie Mary explained that this must be because the fishing fleet was in. Peter, who did not care for fish because of the bones, wished the gulls would swallow the lot. If he was to be deafened by birds and fed on fish he was glad he would only have to stay the one night, bed or no bed.

In the event, apart from a brief and uncomfortable visit home for Christmas and the New Year, Peter was to stay quite a while with Auntie Mary. In her tall stone house he had not only a bed of his own, but a whole room of his own. If he had paid any attention to the talk that had gone on over his head he would have heard that he was to go to school in Aberdeen.

Like his brothers he had walked the three miles to the village school at Lumphanan and sat at the feet of the minister and his wife to learn scripture and his letters; but that was never a regular thing. There was often too much to do at home, scaring the crows or picking the berries or helping with the harvest. Sometimes their boots were at the menders or there was no penny for the lessons. Peter did not care much for the lessons. He had read all the books on the schoolroom shelf and had been given the strap for taking and reading books from the minister's study, so he stayed away after that and played truant as often as he could. But school in Aberdeen was different and he soon found that the more he learned the more they gave him to learn. He was said to be 'a growthy lad' and held his own with boys of eleven and twelve, even though he was a good twelve months younger. Most of the boys were merchants' sons or the sons of sea-going men. Perhaps for that reason the teachers paid special attention to geography and the walls were covered with coloured maps and charts that showed the Baltic trade routes, the Spice Islands, or the shores of the Mediterranean and the North Sea.

The teachers also paid special attention to Peter. Not just because he was a country boy who was poorly dressed, and not just because he was a bright lad. They had plenty of poor scholarship boys, all of them bright and keen to do well. But Peter had a strange way with him of not seeming to care whether he did well or not. He certainly did not see the need to compete for placing with the other boys. Like all the others he called names and pushed and fought, but mostly he went his own way and set his own standards. If he thought he had done something well he would say so and be told off for boasting. If he disagreed with the teachers' opinions he would say so too, and get told off for arrogance. They all complained that he was hard to teach, but they found him quick to learn. Anything and everything new was an adventure and an experience and he was avid for more.

He soon adapted to city life and even grew to like the screams of the gulls that heralded a newly arrived ship. He rarely pined for home or for his mother. Auntie Mary was so different from her sister in every way that it was like living with a stranger – and so they remained, politely and undemandingly estranged. He understood that city life held his certain future from then on.

'One day he'll be a merchant's clerk in a city office, handling parcels of rare goods from the farthest East, won't you Peter?'

'I'll think about it,' he said, and meant it, having learnt the wisdom of paying attention to what was said over his head by members of his family.

18

A merchant's clerk! It might not be such a bad idea. He often passed the time of day with William Shaw who worked as a junior clerk in one of the old, stone warehouses overlooking the harbour. Shaw was a very tall young man of sixteen, who dressed flamboyantly. He had a collection of cravats, one for every day, that his proud mother washed and starched until they crackled like paper. The washing line in his mother's back close was always full of his shirts, his cravats, and his stockings that looked like yellow chicken-legs put out to dry. Peter admired William's wardrobe as unreservedly as he admired the clothes of the merchants who bustled around the harbour: round-faced, Dutch ship-masters with round hats jammed hard on their round heads, to keep their grey wigs from blowing away; seamen of all nations and assorted clothing, who carried bills of lading that they could not read and did not understand; women with lifting, hooped skirts enquiring news of husbands who had sailed months ago for Venice or Virginia or the Hebrides... And the Merchants of Aberdeen! Oh they were fine men, the merchants of Aberdeen. They had fat, white wigs and walked with silver-headed canes. Their embroidered vests were as long as their dark velvet coats, with fine silver buttons only fastened at the waist. Their linen was white and they had silver buckles to fasten the legs of their breeches over their finest Aberdeen stockings.

Peter often went with the other boys from school to meet their fathers on the 'Plainstaines' in Castle street, or the mercat cross. Although he was not accepted in their homes he would stand with the other boys and listen to the talk of commodities and prices and shares and ships. These were the men who shaped the future of the town, who saw that poor boys like Peter got a good schooling, who brought in the trade and paved the roads and cleared the sandbanks in the harbour and managed the affairs of men and ships. They were proud and powerful men, the merchants of Aberdeen. To be a clerk like William Shaw, to serve such men, would be a fine thing – almost as fine as being a merchant himself.

He had no ambition to be a sailor. He had never been on board any of the ships in the harbour. Usually small boys were roughly chased away by the seamen on watch and, to tell the truth, he was afraid of their strange speech and the roughness of the life they led.

He did not know whether he believed half the stories he heard from the other lads and from hanging around the taverns and drinking shops. One day he would go and see for himself, but as a passenger with a proper cabin all to himself, not as a ship's boy sleeping on a pile of ropes in a rat-infested hold below the water-line.

On the whole, after proper consideration, Peter decided that he favoured the life of a clerk like William Shaw. He would marry the merchant's daughter, own ships and trade for himself. What would he trade in? Not fish; he still did not care for fish. No, he would trade in tobacco, spices, wines and fine silks, horn combs, whalebone and whisky. He would travel the world on the deck of his own ship and the captain would call him 'sir'!

Chapter 4

'Well, young sir. Looking for a chance to make your fortune?'

Peter was startled and turned round quickly to see who had spoken.

'You look like a lad who's going to go far.'

He had the biggest bush of wild, red hair that Peter had ever seen. It was tied back in a black bow, but each hair was like fine copper wire and so full of its own energy it would not lie flat. He was a small man with small, nervous hands and small, very dark-brown eyes.

'Wasn't I saying to my friends here... "now there's a lad who's going to go far," I said.'

His friends stood behind him – a man and a boy with a drum. The man had prominent white teeth which were never entirely covered by his very red lips. He breathed noisily through his teeth, almost as though he were trying to whistle some tune which he could not quite remember. The boy seemed older than Peter, but somehow as though he was really a little child inhabiting a large body and finding it a strain. Everything seemed to cost him an effort, and he had to think long and hard before committing himself to some gesture or speech. As if it was something long left undone he rattled a confusion of beats on the drum and grinned happily at the sound of it.

'A very promising young man.'

'Thank you,' Peter said, turning back to the ships. He had walked further than he had intended. Being a Sunday, and early in the year, there were few people about the waterside and he had been full of dreaming.

'A fine fellow like yourself should be looking to make his way in the world, instead of hanging about all on his ownsome.'

The Whistler joined the red-headed man, so that they stood either side of Peter, leaning on the sea-wall. He spoke across Peter's head in a soft, secret voice.

'Bring him to meet the others, Dod. I fancy he'd like fine to meet our other young friends.'

'In a wee while,' said Dod with the copper hair, stretching out his hand to turn Peter away from his sea gazing. 'Have you no friends of your own, young sir? No one to walk with, on a fine, cold Sunday evening?'

'I like being on my own. I'm not a baby.'

'Na, na. I can see that. I ken fine you're a young fella of independent ways... That's the very reason I was saying to mysel' that you might be interested in a little scheme we have in hand.'

The boy beat a furious tattoo on the side-drum and grinned again. Peter felt flustered by this strange trio. He did not fancy being seen in such company. He had a mind that he had seen them before somewhere. Why did they come so close? What did they want from him? Red-headed Dod sounded as though he were trying to sell something at a fairground, something of no value whatsoever.

'A scheme? I've got no money.'

'Wouldn't you like to have money? You could easily earn some.'

'Doing what?'

'What do you do?'

'Nothing. I don't go to work.'

'No work, no friends, all alone in the world. It's a crying shame!'

The Whistler joined in softly, mockingly. 'Where's your mammy, boy? Where's your brothers and sisters? Did they let you out by yourself or did you run off?'

'I live with my Auntie, and she lets me do as I like. I told you I'm not a baby. I'm old enough to take care of myself.'

Dod leaned closer to him. 'He's tied to his Auntie's apron strings! She'd put you to your bed and no supper, I'll be bound, if you were to do some work for us on a Sunday.'

'I do what I like. I'm to be a merchant one day and sail the world.'

Dod looked at the Whistler, who rounded his full, red lips and almost produced a note in surprised reply.

'I told you this was no ordinary young man. We shouldn't make fun of him.' He lowered his voice and drooped his bright head. 'It's such a shame we can't take him with us.'

'Why ever not?' hissed the Whistler out of the side of his mouth.

'He's too young. He lives with his Auntie.'

You mean he's o'er young to make his fortune?'

'Aye, that's the worst of it. All that adventure ... all that wealth ... wasted! Such an opportunity for a young man who wants to be a merchant ... wasted ... forbye the loon's too young!'

Peter had to stand quite close to hear what was said.

'Why?' he asked. 'How old do you have to be? I'm only...'

'Sh!' The Whistler took his shoulder and hissed. Their three heads were quite close now. Only the boy stood apart waiting for the signal words that activated his drum-sticks.

'Don't tell me,' Dod said. 'It'll break my heart if you tell me. I just know you're too young to work: too young to come on board *The Planter*, too young to join our great adventure. Why...' he turned again to the Whistler ... 'I doubt he's old enough to write his own name.'

'I can! I can read and write!'

The Whistler stood up and almost shouted, 'He can read!'

'And write!' Dod waved a signal to the boy, who rat-tatted energetically. 'Here, Jamie, your troubles are over, laddie. Come away ben! This man'll pit your name tae the papers for ye.'

Jamie put down the drum carefully and slowly, crossed the sticks on top, wiped his hands on his breeks and ambled over to stand beside Peter. Dod took Peter's arm encouragingly.

'Now then young man, would you defy your auntie and help this laddie out of a wee difficulty he has? It's not such hard work and you'd earn yourself a penny or two. It's just to do a bit of writing.'

'Of course, I'd be glad to help.'

'You see, there's not many can read and write the way you can, and we need someone to show us the way.'

Peter looked up at Jamie's face. The boy was even bigger than he thought. His wrists were inches out of the cuffs of his shirt, and although it was January, and a raw, damp evening with the mists already creeping up, his legs were bare and the heels of his shoes all trodden down as if his feet were too big. Jamie nodded encouragingly at Peter. His eyes were bright with anticipation. He licked his lips and rubbed his breeks again as if to polish the palms of his hands against his buttocks.

23

'Could you show him how you write your own name first? Just so's he gets the drift of it.'

Peter was handed a steel nibbed pen and Dod held out a small old-fashioned ink-bottle made from a cow's horn. From a satchel that he had been wearing under his coat the Whistler produced a piece of paper and folded it across the centre. Selecting a flat stone on the sea wall he laid the paper down and spread his hand across it to hold it from blowing away.

'There you are. Now, Jamie, you watch and this young man will show you how he writes his name, and then maybe he'll help you to write yours.'

Jamie stood, breathing heavily over the paper, as if the writing was about to appear all by itself. Peter dipped the pen in the ink-horn and, carefully, so that Jamie could see how it was done, he wrote his own name – Peter Williamson – on the damp, folded paper.

*

The next few hours felt like drowning. Drowning over and over again. No sooner did he surface from one overwhelming feeling than he was plunged into another one. The moment his own name glared up at him from the stone of the sea wall his arms were wrenched behind and he was abruptly dragged away. A conjuror could not have acted more dextrously. Paper, ink-horn, drum and all: everything vanished.

For a moment Peter kept his hold on the situation. 'What about Jamie? I haven't written his name!'

'He'll get by.'

Dod shoved the drum against Jamie's chest and, as if by doing that he had pressed some sort of spring, the boy's gangling arms sprang up to encircle it and to hold it to him: a precious thing, his belonging. He put the strap over his head, picked up the sticks and slopped along behind the three of them. Although he was bawling like a calf, with tears rushing down his cheeks, Jamie battered away, without rhythm and without sense all the way to the barn.

Peter did not cry, but went down under a great, black wave of shame. He had been duped! Duped, tricked, set up, and tumbled in the mire. A moment ago he had been so superior, so grand. The educated young gentleman who had felt nothing but pity for poor, daft Jamie; who had flourished a pen, showed his skill – put his name to a paper, and signed himself up for goodness knows what villainy!

'What are you doing? Where are you taking me?' The Whistler squeezed the muscles of his upper arm so that he cried out. His feet were almost off the ground. He was floundering … drowning. 'Let me go!'

There were people at the end of the street – a shawled goodwife and her cronies, pausing for a while in the damp chill to gossip on the corner. 'Help!' They looked up at the strange group coming towards them. 'Help!'

'Run off, did he?'

'A limb of Satan. Look what he did to that poor unfortunate boy there. Look how he made him cry. A good thrashing is what he'll get.'

'That's right, Mister. Warm his backside for him!'

'Just you pay attention to your daddie, young man; he knows what's best for you.'

Their voices blew back down the street as Peter's captors faced into the wind and ran him away from Ship Row and headed for the Green.

The wave of shame receded, leaving only red anger pushing against his eyes. Suspended between Red Dod and the Whistler, kick and struggle though he might, he could not get loose. They were neither of them big men, but they kept up such a brisk pace that they were across the strip of scrubby grass that gave the Green its name and at the door of the barn without him landing a single blow.

Sitting on a wooden box outside the barn door was a hugely fat man, wrapped in a plaid. His paunch rested on his knees, half covering a whip of plaited leather that dangled there. When he saw the whip, Peter gave up struggling, for now he remembered where he had seen two of these men before. That time there had been a small difference, for then Dod had been the little man high-stepping with the drum and the Whistler had been the whipper-in, behind the pack of women and girls at Michael Fair, more than a year ago. What was it the carrier had said? 'Inviting people to go abroad with them.' Inviting! He had not accepted their invitation.

'What've you got there, Farquharson?' asked the fat man, wheezing

25

with laughter so that his belly shook. 'Toss it back in the watter, man; it's no but a puddock wi' kickin' legs!'

The Whistler, whose name was Farquharson, sucked his breath through his teeth. 'Oh it's a toad'll hop fine, when it's learnt some manners. It's called Peter McWilliam. Put him with the other boys and watch out for him.'

Red Dod put his hand under the skirt of the Whistler's coat and pulled out the paper Peter had signed.

'Here's his indentures. This one signed up like a lamb. His name's Peter Williamson, not McWilliam. He's no' a highlander, are you laddie?'

'Williamson, McWilliam, same difference. Lowland or Highland, Inland or Island, he'll still be worth money. This one can read and write!' The Whistler pulled Peter away from Dod, and, smiling his toothy grin, he bent over so that his face was only inches away from Peter's nose, and hissed, 'You're worth money, do you understand, Peter Whatever-your-name-is. You've signed yourself over, and you belong to us.' He straightened up. 'Put him in the book, Mister Jeffrey, and mind you keep him safe.'

'Oh, I'll watch him, don't you fret.' Mr Jeffrey, the fat man, fingered the handle of the snaky whip and turned his eyes towards Peter. The flesh of his face spread in huge mountains upwards and outwards from his round, pale nose, so that his eyes seemed to have no lids, no eyelashes! 'Put him inside. I'll watch him for you.'

The Whistler gave Peter a push so that he fell backwards into the dark where the barn door stood open a space. Before he could scramble to his feet he heard the door close, and the bar that held it drop into iron sockets. He was a prisoner!

Chapter 5

Lurching and stumbling, he made for the place where the door was. It was not so dark in the barn once you got used to it; there were plenty of holes and chinks in the wooden walls. Peter attacked the door with fists and with feet. It shook and rattled but it sounded heavy and solid as he pounded on it. His voice slid feebly over the huge spread of rough, damp timber. What use was shouting? Few people had cause to come down on to the Green. The grass was poor and salty, especially in winter; no fit grazing, not even for geese, and there were few buildings out this side of the city.

Exhausted, Peter sank onto his knees. He gave up the attempt to shout and bowed himself forward, hugging his bruised fists against his stomach. The barn seemed to be full of birds: he could hear squeaks and flapping, and rustling in the corners. Bats! Was the barn full of bats? He did not care at all for that idea.

He screamed out loud as something brushed against his hunched shoulders. The bats were about to attack and suck out his blood!

'Whisht there, I'll not hurt you.'

He could not see. Was someone there? Relief and panic warmed and chilled him in quick succession. Not bats then, since they do not talk. Ghosts! It must be ghosts. Spirits in a haunted barn on a deserted green.

'Are you a spirit?'

The ghost giggled. It was a very human giggle.

'Oh, aye. Spirited, like yourself.'

'I'm not dead.'

'Nor'm I, but I am to be spirited. Did you sign?

'I was tricked.'

'You did sign.'

'I put my name to something. I don't know what it was.'

He could see her now in the faint, grey light of the barn. She was a brown girl – brown hair, brown skin, brown dress. In an attempt at finery she had piled her hair up on top of her head and, in the absence of a comb, tied it with a narrow strip of lace.

'Ay, you signed your name, like all the rest. Mine's Kirsty. What's yours?'

'Peter. What's going on? When do we get out?'

'You don't know? Why? Are you a country boy?'

'I am not! I live here.' He saw no reason for telling this scornful creature that he was in truth a country boy, that he was almost a stranger here, lost and frightened.

'How old are you?'

Should he lie? Say he was fourteen? 'Eleven,' he mumbled miserably.

'You're big for your age. That'll be why they took you. Come over here.'

She dragged him to his feet. She was strong: a sort of half-woman girl, like Jeannie, and, like Jeannie, used to giving orders. She had said she was a spirit, yet the hand leading him was warm and plump, and, for all he could see in the semi-darkness, she cast a shadow as substantial as his own.

'Here, it's out of the draught.' As she caught hold of his arm, he winced and drew away. 'Did they hurt you?'

'My arm's a bit sore. They held me up, so my feet couldn't touch the ground.'

'It was William Farquharson took you, wasn't it? He's aye rough. Who was the other one? Do you know?'

'A red-headed man – I think they call him "Dod" – and a boy with a drum.'

'Oh that'll be George Lunen, and the boy – he's a spirit too – James Ingram his name is. "Daft Jamie".'

All this talk of spirits was unnerving. Peter felt sick and dizzy; he wanted to lie down; he wanted time to take in all this cold strangeness.

'What ails you? When did you eat last?'

'I had breakfast. Then I went walking. I'll have missed my dinner.'

'The others will be here soon. They left me and Janet here; she's not been well so I said I'd stay to keep an eye on her. When the others come back it'll be fine and noisy and there'll be dancing and plenty to eat. Sit here on the side before you fade away. There's some milk put by for Janet. She'll not mind if I give you some to tide you over.'

Peter was getting used to the gloom and could see that there were boxes and bundles piled against the wall and dozens of dirty-white blankets heaped on the straw. The end wall of the barn was stone and it was warmer here. Kirsty brought milk from a can that stood on a trestle table. Then he saw Janet lying nearby, wrapped in a blanket. For a moment it was as if a cold hand clutched at his stomach; at her side on the blanket was a small, tightly wrapped bundle. The woman lay so still it was as if he saw again the image of his mother, in the big bed at home, her dead baby beside her.

'Is she dead?' he whispered.

'Of course not, stupid. She had a fever and the baby did not thrive for a while, but now she's fine. You must have heard the wean whimpering when they ... when you came.'

Peter thought of the squeaking and rustling he had taken to be birds and said nothing. He was not going to admit that he had been afraid.

'Is the baby to be spirited too?'

'Oh, aye, mother and son; they'll both be spirited when the time comes. She has no husband to be a father to the boy. She hopes maybe to find one in the New World, though at this rate the wean will be grown before ever we sail.'

Peter sat silent, letting her prattle on, sipping the milk and listening – listening to all the terrible things she was saying so gaily, so carelessly.

'Two ships they have waiting and the owners desperate for folks to enlist. Last year and the year before, what with the poor harvest and the hard living, hundreds signed up for twenty-one years in the plantations, but this winter there's meal a-plenty and folks would rather bide at home.'

'Twenty-one years! Did you say twenty-one years?'

'Sh! You'll wake the bairn again. Four years, seven years, depending on your age of course. The younger you are, the longer you serve.'

He sunk his nose into the beaker. There was no milk left but he did not trust himself to speak, for fear his voice would tremble and give him away. He had signed his name on a bit of paper. The top part had been folded down. *What was on that paper?*

29

Chapter 6

Whether he was stunned by what had happened, or whether there was something besides milk in the beaker, Peter lay back in the straw, beside the sick woman and the sleeping child. Kirsty had disappeared somewhere, into the gloom. He was not asleep, but everything seemed very far away, as if it was happening to someone else. He knew now that he had been tricked into signing up to work on the Plantations, but what that implied he had no idea. He thought back over what Kirsty had said. The Plantations were in the New World, he knew that much. In school they had learnt about Walter Raleigh and Francis Drake, and the English colonies along the coast of America. He knew that ships from Scotland crossed the Atlantic ocean, bringing tobacco, sugar, and the beaver furs that were felted into the fine, black hats the merchants of Aberdeen wore with such assurance.

He was less sure about the outward journey. Convicts. He knew that convicted men and women were shipped to the New World. He had never seen them taken from the tollbooth, laden with chains and led on board, but he knew such things happened. Criminals, who had committed terrible and wicked crimes, were condemned to hard labour overseas. That was right and proper. Once they had worked their punishment they would be set free on the other side of the world, out of harm's way. There was no coming back, so the country was well rid of them. If they did not lead honest, Christian lives, then let them bide with savages! It was kinder than hanging them, out beyond the town on Gallows Hill. Everybody said so. But he was not a criminal. Oh, to be sure, he was no angel. He'd done his share of fighting, and he had stolen before now – from the larder at home, books from the manse – but he had returned those. Surely that was not enough to convict him a felon?

Auntie Mary had said to the carrier that poor men sold their children. Was Father so poor? Did they want to be rid of him? Was that why they'd sent him away? Another mouth to feed, a growing body to be clothed? But there had always been food on the table at home, and clothes to wear – second-hand, third-hand, cut down from the older boys, but always clean clothes on Sundays.

Was it because he used to run off? But that was over a year ago. Now he was a scholar, hardly a day missed from Robert Gordon's School. They watched out for truants, they would send out to find him; Auntie Mary would miss him from supper; it was all a mistake; he would explain to them that he was neither a criminal nor a runaway and they would send him home – when they came with the evening meal... He closed his eyes and stretched himself in the straw that was warm and smelled of the country...

*

The party that burst into the barn was like no other that Peter had ever known. Night and dark had come early from the sea mist, and even the gull-laden air was damped down and heavy. Yet these revellers were as rosy and noisy as if it were spring. Men and women, boys and girls, they swept through the great door of the barn, a piper all out of breath and out of tune in the midst. Daft Jamie was there too, frowning and groaning and banging away at his drum like a soutar mending shoes. They brought lanterns and a small handcart laden with baskets of loaves and oatcakes, and great lidded pans packed about with hay. They lifted the lids off the pans, and steam, smelling of mutton and turnips, of barley and onions, came rolling towards Peter, making his mouth water and his nose run. Oh, but he was hungry and these were the happiest souls he had seen since he came to this city!

In a moment Janet was propped up, smiling and looking fine in the gold lantern-light; one of the other women had the babe on her knee and was spooning warm gruel into its tiny, pink mouth and over its small, pink chin, and Kirsty was beside him, dragging him to his feet.

'Come away, Peter. Here's the others returned and supper on the table.'

He pulled back from her. This was all very fine but he was here because of a mistake. He should try to explain it to someone. Someone should be told.

'I should be getting home just now. There's supper waiting for me at my auntie's.'

'Peter, you must still be half asleep. You're one of us now. They'll not let you go.'

'But it's all a mistake. You don't understand! I'm not a criminal, and my family is not so poor that they must sell me, like a pig to the market. I don't want to go to the Plantations anyway.'

'Peter, I know that, but look there.' She pointed towards the doorway. Just out of the lantern light, but clearly visible against the grey sky outside, were three men. One was immensely fat, one had a bush of red hair and one sounded as though he were trying to whistle some half-remembered tune through his teeth.

Peter allowed himself to be dragged over to the trestle table. A bowl of stew, a lump of bread and a spoon were put into his hand, and he sat with Kirsty and Jamie, who had lumbered over to join them. The stew was good and he was hungry. He supposed that this was an adventure. He was certain that Auntie Mary and the dominie at the school would seek him out in the morning, and he did not fancy explaining their mistake to the three villains at the door, just now. Maybe later. After all he could send a message, or go himself when they sent him out with the others. He cleaned his plate and wiped up the gravy with a piece of the bread.

Another boy brought his plate over. He seemed about Kirsty's age. He had a ragged thatch of straw-coloured hair and was grinning all over his freckled face. He flumped down beside Jamie, making him choke on the breadcrumbs; then, in order to cure the choking, he thumped him so hard on the back that he spilt his stew all down his outgrown breeches and had to go for more. After that, all three of them had to throw out the straw with stew spilt on it and Kirsty had to complain about the boy's behaviour, so that it was a while before they all sat peacefully together. Jamie wolfed down the stew, and the freckled boy made himself known.

His name was also Peter, Peter Kemp, but he was known as 'Stookie' from the shock of straw-like hair that stood up from his head. He had signed up with George Lunen cheerfully and was keen to get

32

away. He was even happy about the idea of travelling with convicts.

'They come on board ship in chains, but once in the New World they get a fresh start. Oh, for sure they have to serve their time, just like us, but after that they're free men. They'll have a good life. It's better than hanging.'

'Aye, mebbe. But how can they get back?'

'I'll not come back. Never. Not on your life. What's here to come home to? Scratching a living from the stones? Ploughing the furrows of the sea for a few caller herring? Out there . . .' He waved generously towards the door and the sea . . . 'There, you can throw a basket overboard and draw it in full of cod! Time after time! You don't have to follow the shoals up and down, up and down the long coastline. There the rivers and seas on your own doorstep are brimming over with food.'

Kirsty joined in. 'What's here for most people, Peter? Hard toil for a hard master. We'll have to expect that too, at first, all of us, while we're young and learning new ways. But after that . . . Peter, you'll have your own land and ride in a carriage with servants of your own!'

'Eat sugar and drink wine!'

Peter was taken completely by surprise. He had thought that Jamie could not, or did not, speak. Yet here he was shouting at the top of his voice. His speech was somewhat thick, as though his lips and tongue were clumsy like the rest of his movements. But his voice was strong and powerful.

Stookie roared with laughter and tumbled Jamie in the straw. Though Jamie was the bigger of the two he allowed himself to be buried, pummelled and tickled by Stookie. 'You're right there, Jamie. Eat sugar, Jamie; drink red wine, Jamie and live like a laird, Jamie; wi' lands of your ain!'

'Peter Kemp, you are a gowk!' Kirsty gathered up her skirts from the struggling boys. 'He'll wet himself if you tickle him like that. Let him catch his breath while we put the dishes to be washed.'

The four young people gathered the crocks together and dusted the straw off themselves. The piper was filling his bag ready for the dancing: the benches on which many of the older men and women had been sitting at table, were pushed back to make a clear space, and people were beginning to form sets for the first reel. Peter had never been light on his feet, but he loved watching other people dance, and he had an ear for music of all kinds.

When they came looking for him in the morning he would be able to say that he had behaved like a man. Maybe he had been taken in and made a fool of, but it had been an experience. His new friends had set him thinking. He needed to make decisions. Should he hold to his ambition of becoming a merchant's clerk in the busy trade of a shipping town? Or should he rather become a landowner in unknown lands across the sea? The folk around him seemed happy enough. The winding and unwinding of the dance made bright patterns in the barn. He could see Kirsty, her brown skirts swinging, her cheeks rosy with the exertion. Some of the men had tobacco in long-stemmed pipes and both men and women had whisky enough to loosen their laughter and their singing voices. They had made their choice. Like Stookie, they had signed for their future. Beyond the dancing, against the dark doorway stood Farquharson, the Whistler, and for some reason Peter was reminded of a children's game they used to play at home; it had words to it:

> Will you buy syboes? Will you buy leeks?
> Will you buy my bonnie lassie wi' the red cheeks?
>
> I'll not buy syboes, I'll not buy leeks
> But I'll buy your bonnie lassie wi' the red cheeks.

He shivered and turned away to where Jamie stood watching the dancers with shining eyes.

Chapter 7

The next morning began bright and clear. Monday morning: people going to work, carts trundling in from the West Gate along the Green, laden with fern and hay and turnips. To the folk in the barn it seemed like a holiday. No hurry to get up and go to work. There was a lazy rustling and stretching in the straw. Women went to fetch water to wash themselves and their clothes. A bustling, motherly creature, with a couple of boys in attendance, brought more of the hay boxes with pots of hot porridge in them. Her name, he found, was Helen Law, and she was paid to feed and care for the 'servants' as they were called.

Peter learned a good deal about the people in the barn, that Monday morning. Most, he discovered, had taken out legitimate indentures to serve as field hands or house servants on the tobacco plantations or farms in the New World. They were confident in the certainty that the trade in tobacco was on the increase and that, after a term of unpaid work, they would be given a start towards getting land of their own.

Nobody seemed either to believe or to pay any attention to his story of having been tricked into signing. They were on holiday; they were off on an adventure of their own choosing; they were grateful to the men who kept them so carefully and gave them free food and shelter.

'Why do they watch us all the time?' Peter asked one man, a carpenter by trade, who boasted that he had his own tools and would be sure of work in a land where there were so many trees.

'To prevent folk running off.'

'But if they want to go, they surely wouldn't run away, would they?'

'There's always some who'll take advantage of others. Why last year, so I'm told, there was some young men took a notion to make a bit o' siller, so they upped and went to one of these agents and, "Here's these fellas for the New World," says one of them. "What'll you give me for bringing them to you?" "One shillin' and six pence," says the agent. "Each," says the young man. And so he signs them up and they come down and stay on board the ship for a day or two, and then the one finds he has forgotten his tools at home and the other has to go and visit his grannie, and for one reason and another they go ashore, promising to return the same day. Well, what do you think they do? Why, they go straight off to another agent. He gives two shilling each, so they sign on with him.'

'Why do the agents pay people? I thought they *wanted* to go?'

'It's like sealing the bargain. They pay some small sum when you sign, then it's in the book and legal, and they guarantee to feed you while you're waiting to sail, so then your new master buys back your indentures from them on the other side.'

'How much do they pay?'

'You're o'er fond of asking questions, are you not? Let's see, a lad like you would fetch ten – mebbe twelve – pound. How old are ye?'

'Eleven.'

'Well, you'd fetch ... how old did you say?'

'Eleven.'

'Well, I'd be careful not to tell, if I were you.'

'Why not?'

'You should not have signed. It's like joining the king's army. They'll not take you under fourteen years.'

'But I didn't want to go. I was forced to.'

'They would never do that. It's against the law. The papers go to a magistrate.'

'But I was, Mister. They asked me to show how I could write my name. If you don't believe me, ask Jamie. James Ingram. He was there!'

'Daft Jamie? Pay no attention to him, he's not right in the head. They'll have trouble finding a place for him – although, even if he is slow, I suppose he's willing enough.'

'I'm not willing enough. I want to go home.'

'Oh, they all get homesick for their mammy some time. You'll get over it.'

Peter gave up after that.

Apart from the four young people and the baby there were fifteen or so men and women in the barn. All of them seemed glad to go and nobody regarded him as any different from themselves, even if they said they believed his story. He began to think himself as daft as Jamie. Who would believe a boy daft enough to be taken in by a trick like that? The only hope lay in someone coming to look for him.

He knew it would be some days before anyone would think of enquiring at the barn, so he held his peace about being tricked and went to join Stookie and Kirsty.

That afternoon they were allowed out as far as the burn that ran into the sea, to play at ball. Everyone that could joined in a mad scramble and running battle for possession of the ball. It was like no game Peter had ever seen. There seemed to be two teams of men and girls who ran and fought and teased and laughed in the salty mudflats at the edge of the sea. There were birds here of all kinds, none of which Peter recognized. They screamed and teased and fought too and the air was full of desperate sounds: crying, laughing, water hissing against sour reeds, footsteps splashing and the thin soughing of the wind. Peter stood back from the game, out of breath and feeling close to tears.

As always they were kept under guard: on the bridge over the Denn Burn were the usual two men with whips. As Peter watched, he saw one of them run down towards the players and, for a moment, it looked as though he wanted to join in. It was still cold, even though the wind was small and the sea calm; perhaps he was cold on the bridge and wanted a run. He was shouting too, over the cries of the birds, and no-one passed him the ball. The game stopped. The players stood there, dishevelled, their arms hanging loose, heaving for breath, all laughter gone. Slowly they picked their way back towards Peter, the man Jeffrey cracking his whip to hurry them along.

On the road over the bridge came a small party of men and women, hurrying, purposeful, waving papers and pointing towards the players on the strand.

'It's my Fayther!' Jamie bellowed in his strange, suddenly loud voice. He began to gallop lop-sidedly towards the bridge. But before Peter was fully aware of what was happening, a dark snake slapped through the air across Jamie's neck bringing him to a crying halt. Immediately, there was a hubbub amongst the others on the strand. Angrily they surrounded Jamie, trying to comfort the howling boy, shaking their fists at Jeffrey who had lashed him.

There were angry shouts too from the men on the bridge as the players were herded towards the barn, joined by their other jailers. Jamie was still howling in his cracked voice, although Kirsty had her arm round him, and Peter looked for Stookie to come to Jamie's aid. When he caught sight of him he almost did not recognise the boy who had joked and laughed the night before. He was walking backwards, shouting and stumbling, his face twisted with anger and grief. A soberly dressed man in a black coat, with a tall, thin-faced woman on his arm, was trying to break past the fat man to get near him.

'Peter Kemp, come here to me at once! That's my son ... Peter Kemp. You have no right to keep us from him! I have papers here.'

It was not until they were inside the barn that there was a moment for anything other than confused shouting and the cracking of whips. Then the three guards turned to face the small group of angry parents, led by Stookie's father.

'Give me back my son. You have no right to take him.'

'Ah, but you're wrong there, Mister,' said Dod Lunen, purring as quiet as a kitten. 'He has signed indentures to go as a servant.'

'I know that, but we have rights too. He's our son and we do not want him to go. He's to join me in my profession as house-painter.'

'We refuse permission,' joined in Mrs Kemp.

'You will be the mother, I presume,' he purred again. 'The boy said it was by cause of your ill treatment that he wished to leave home. Did you know that, Mrs Kemp?'

'A mother may chastise her son once in a while,' broke in Stookie's father, indignantly, 'and if she beat him black and blue, he is still our son and I have a writ here from a magistrate saying he must be returned to me this instant.' He held out the stiff, expensive paper for all to see. 'There it is, signed by Mr Seton. I'd to go far afield for this. Now will you let him go!'

Now it was Jamie's father who joined in. He was an elderly, bowed figure in threadbare clothes and wearing a knitted cap. 'It's kidnapping,' he said several times. 'It's kidnapping. Why, my boy there is not able to read nor write, so how can you say he signed his name to anything? You have trepanned him, as the saying goes. What you have done... It is not at all right; trepanning is not right at all. His mother is fair demented. We fetched him away once and took him home, and you people came and fetched him from his bed, and carried him away with nothing but his shirt!'

Dod Lunen stepped forward, brushing Mr Ingram aside, and spoke to the group of parents. What he said was cold, flat and quite, quite final.

'Everyone here is here legally. We have done everything according to law. We have legal papers attested by magistrates, for every person in this place. Now take yourselves off and leave us alone.'

There was a moment's silence and then everyone began to shout at once. Peter crept up to the side of the door where he could see more clearly. Perhaps when his auntie had missed him last night she had sent someone out to look for him, but among the angry crowd there was no face he recognized. Above the noise, Mr Kemp made himself heard once more.

'By law you say, sir. Then by law, and with these papers of authority, I wish to purchase my son's release from his indentures. I believe the proper sum is sixteen shillings.' He drew out a small leather bag from his coat pocket.

Peter looked at Stookie, who was tense and white with anger. 'I'll not stand for it! I'm not a parcel of goods to be handed over for cash. I'm going away to seek my fortune. I'll not stand for it!'

As Stookie neared the door it opened further, although no more light came in, for the space was filled by the enormous bulk of Mr Jeffrey, who reached a massive arm towards the boy and dragged him into the open. Beyond his bulk Peter could hear the fairground tones of Dod Lunen, no purring now, addressing the crowd.

'There you are, good people! You can see for yourselves, we do not force people to break the law in any way. This young man signed to go to the Plantations and to make his fortune. But his father has every right to deny his son the privilege if he so wishes. Anyone may buy themselves out of an apprenticeship if they can get a magistrate to contract them out of their legal obligations. Any one at all. But without such papers, I'm afraid the law must be maintained. There is an agreement in force between us, and no-one can go back on his word.'

All this while Stookie was held tightly against the massive thighs of the fat man. But, when Dod had finished his fine speech, Mr Jeffrey pushed him forward so that he stumbled into his father's arms. Peter had only one glimpse of his straw-coloured hair, gripped tight beneath his father's elbow, before the barn door was barred shut and everything was dark again. There was still some shouting outside but it soon died away and only Daft Jamie's hiccoughing sobs and some disgruntled murmuring from the other folk in the barn could be heard above the wind whistling through the timbers.

That night there was no dancing and the piper only played laments. When the food was brought and the hay boxes opened, and the warm, comforting smells filled the barn, people ate and were satisfied; but it was no party, and the whisky drinking and card playing were in small groups around lanterns set upon boxes and barrels. The joy and adventure had gone, and Peter, Kirsty and Jamie settled down to sleep in a deadening silence. Peter was surprised how tired he felt. The short winter day had been even shorter than usual because they had got up so late, but he felt as though he had been ploughing uphill, he was so worn with emotion and so stunned at losing the boy who had so quickly become a friend.

In spite of feeling tired, he could not sleep. The straw prickled and felt lumpy; Jamie thrashed and muttered at his side, sleeping untidily in a mess of old sacks and bits of blanket. Peter longed for his neat, narrow bed at Aunt Mary's, for the pallet he had shared with his brothers at home, for anything away from this place. The top of his stomach tightened in great, gulping sobs and, as quietly as he could, for fear of Kirsty waking up to pity him, Peter Williamson finally cried himself to sleep.

Chapter 8

It was hardly light the next morning when they came to take them away. The women were taken off in one group into the care of Helen Law, the men went into the tollbooth with the convicts, and into the workhouse which was conveniently next door, and the boys were put into a tall, thin house with a large door in front and a high-walled yard at the back. The house was up a narrow close by the workhouse and Peter thought they might just as well be in the workhouse or in the prison itself, for the windows were small and high and the doors had new locks on them.

He spent the next few days cooped up in that house, frustrated, knowing he couldn't get away; for the boys were watched over day and night. They were not ill-treated: the food was plentiful, they slept on straw pallets and the blankets were clean. Peter was given a change of clothes and had his head washed with tar soap in case of lice. He was certainly the youngest boy there; the others were all in their teens and anxious to get away to start a new life.

Without Stookie and Kirsty to depend on for friendship and protection, Peter and Jamie were thrust more and more into each other's company. Jamie had been given a pair of shoes which, although they were not new, were certainly better than the old ones. Like Peter, he too had new stockings and this almost made up to him for the loss of the drum and the freedom of the streets with Dod and the Whistler. Peter tried to teach him to write his name with the charred end of a piece of firewood, and soon the walls were covered with crooked Js and attempts at 'Ingram' made with much heavy breathing, and Peter's guiding hand. After a while, however, they were made to scrub the writing off and Peter doubted if Jamie would ever be able to sign his name or do more than set his mark or thumbprint on any papers. He began to doubt whether reading or writing were of any value. Here was he, a scholar from Gordon's school, no better off than Jamie, or any of the other lads, snared by his writing into being a servant in some wild convict country over the ocean. This was not how he had imagined spending his manhood. It was a far cry from a future of counting bales of cotton and bundles of tobacco leaf in an Aberdeen warehouse, to be forced to go out and grow the stuff, bent double in the hot sun, under the threat of whips and punishment. He was not taken in by Jamie's cries of 'Drink wine and eat sugar!' nor the other boys' calculation that the reason no-one ever came back was that they all got rich over there and had plantations of their own. Peter was none so easily persuaded.

He learnt that they were waiting for two things to happen. They needed more people before it was worthwhile sending out a ship, and they needed an exceptionally high tide, a neap tide, to take Captain Ragg's ship *The Planter* over the sand bank at Tory and onto the high seas.

The waiting and the boredom affected everyone. Even the older boys were talking about going home. There were now eight young men in the house, counting Peter and Jamie; three more had been brought in by a saddler of the name of Smith, and like him, these were large, rough fellows. Peter and Jamie tried to keep away from them as much as possible, but it was difficult with them penned so close, and only allowed out into the yard for an airing. These boys very quickly got the measure of Jamie and teased him and made him slave for them. Peter was constantly amazed at how he would grovel and bow to them in an exaggerated imitation of humility. He would do whatever they asked of him. If they said 'Eat dirt!' he would eat dirt. Peter tried to scold him into standing up for himself, but Jamie only mopped and mowed to him, wrung his great hands and cried. Then Peter fought for Jamie himself, punching and kicking and using fine words, like the monitors did on the bad boys at school, but they only laughed and knocked him down and hurt his arms and twisted his ears, so that, after a while, he found that the best way to protect his friend was to follow Jamie's example, humbling himself and bearing their insults and ill-treatment in silence. If they forgot about him, if he was canny enough to keep out of the way, then he could help Jamie in the tasks he was given and even prevent him being bullied and beaten when he made a mess of things.

When they had been in the house about four or five days the lads got Jamie to make a hole in the wall of the yard. There was a new man on guard – a pleasant, soft-voiced man called James Robertson. He seemed to have no connection with the others but to have been employed to watch over them. This afternoon he was sitting at ease with a pipe, after eating his lunch. Two of the lads kept him in conversation whilst the others stood around watching as Jamie demolished the wall. Peter felt he had to help Jamie, although for the life of him he could not see what fun they got from watching a poor, daft lad tearing his fingernails, already bitten to the quick, to pieces on the rough stones.

They had made quite a sizeable gap at the top of the wall, and, in so doing, produced a pile of loose stones and rubble at the bottom, when they were pushed roughly aside and three of the older boys scrambled over the gap and into the narrow close at the back. Peter suddenly saw a chance to get away.

'Jamie! Come on! We'll go too.'

'No.'

'Yes, Jamie. We'll run off and find our folks. It's easy.'

'No.'

'Why not? I'll take you to my Auntie's.'

'Promised not to.'

'I can't go without you. Come on! You've got to.'

Peter dragged Jamie to the hole and pushed him over, then scrambled up himself, grazing his knees and elbows. He was smaller than the others and the hole was still high above him. Jamie had slithered through and dropped down on to his hands and knees in the alley-way. Peter was afraid of landing on top of him, so waited a moment, on top of the wall, for him to get to his feet. There was a gate, further down the close and he could see the young men going through it. They were laughing and kicking up a racket, which seemed odd, if they were trying to make an escape. Anyway, why didn't they go straight down to the end, where there was a wide street full of folk and friendly comings and goings.

'Look out Jamie, I'm coming.'

It was a very long way down the other side, and he hesitated to jump, but he was just about to push himself off into space when a rough hand grabbed the top of his breeches and held him firm.

'Oh no, laddie. Not this time, you don't!'

It was Mr Robertson who dragged him backwards out of the gap, held him like a baby, with his feet in the air for a second, and then dumped him, none too gently, on the hard paving of the yard.

'Where's yon daft yin? Did he do all this?' He climbed up the pile of stones to look for Jamie. 'Come you here at once, James Ingram, or I'll fetch Dod to ye wi' the big stick.'

Peter could hear Jamie whimpering on the far side of the wall.

'He can't get back by himself, it's too high.'

'Well now, you just stay right where you are James Ingram, and I'll come round and fetch you.' Robertson called out, much less angrily, and turned to Peter. 'As for you, Peter Williamson, I'll shut you in the cellar, whilst I round up those other young stirks. Now come with me and no more of your tricks.'

All this time Peter had sat where he was dumped, on the ground. As he scrambled to his feet, he thought he heard his name being called.

'Jamie,' he shouted. 'It's all right, Jamie. It's not your fault. Just stay where you are.'

'Peter! Is that you? It's Alex. I've come to find you!'

'Alex? Where are you?' Peter dodged round Robinson's arm and rushed for the gap in the wall. 'Have you come to get me out? Is Father with you?'

He could see Alex now, far below in the alley. There was only Jamie with him. It was too far. He would never be able to reach him. He would have to jump the wall. He would have to fly! Oh Alex! Mr Robertson was just behind him... He kicked out wildly and threw himself at the wall. He tried to jump, or even to fall through the gap, but it was no use; Robertson had hold of his ankle and was pulling him down. He could no longer see either his brother or poor daft Jamie in the lane, only the dark grey stone of the wall that kept them out and kept him prisoner.

'I'll fetch Father. He'll get you away. Don't fret yoursel'. We'll have you away home in no time, no time at all!'

'Is that your brother? Why don't we fetch him to go to the New World along of yourself? I'll be sure he's a fine young fella like yourself.'

'Alex! Run! Don't let them get you too. Get Father to get papers

44

from the magistrate. Tell him he'll need money!' Robertson was peering over the wall at Alex now. It would never do if he were taken as well. 'Go on, Alex. Tell Auntie where I am. I didn't want to go. They made me sign. Don't let them catch you too. Get Father! Go on!'

He was dragged into the house. Robertson did not put him into the cellar, but locked him in, nonetheless, while he went to fetch the others. It seemed that the older lads had just gone visiting. They had called on the women who were boarded with Helen Law. The gate that Peter had seen led from the close to her back yard and it was nothing but a dare had led them to climb out and 'pay their respects' to the women servants. It seemed that it was only Peter who was fool enough to want to escape. 'Everyone else,' they told him, 'was satisfied with their good fortune! Most people would consider them the luckiest folk in the world to be fed and boarded and have free passage to the New World! It was just that they had had to wait a little longer than usual, but just think how lucky they were! Tomorrow they were to be moved again! Tomorrow they were to be taken on board *The Planter*. No more being cooped up in the town. Tomorrow they would be in the fresh air of the harbour at Tory, away from all outside interference.

'Interference! That means Alex. They're afraid he'll bring help next time. How will he ever find me now?'

That night he took another stick from the fire. This time he wrote his own name: 'Peter Williamson, *The Planter*, Tory' on the wall behind the door, where it might pass notice in the morning. He had no real hope that Alex would see it, unless he could get into the house, and unless he thought to look behind the door, but it made him feel better to leave some record behind, something to show that he had once been there. He added one more word. Above his name he wrote 'Spirited'. Then he rolled himself in his blanket to sleep, because tomorrow he was going to sea.

Chapter 9

Peter woke in tears. He was not sure why he was crying. It had something to do with a dream, but he could not remember what the dream was about. He was still wrapped like a sausage-roll in his blanket next to Jamie who reached out to squeeze his shoulder in rough, silent comforting.

'It's all my fault. If I hadn't called out to my brother, if I hadn't asked him to bring Father; if I had been like you Jamie, and held my whisht, none of this would have happened.'

Peter knew that a move to the ships would be certain to prevent any hope of his family finding him. They were country folk, what did they know about ships? Besides, his father had to work. How could he leave Hirnley to hunt for a schoolboy son who was forever running away!

He shifted and turned over, wrapping himself tighter in the bedclothes. There was a glimmer of light in the window; it would soon be morning.

There was no chance of getting back to sleep, however. The next moment he was sent sprawling out of his cocoon. He had no need to ask who it was who had tipped him out; he could hear the whistling breath that sounded almost like a tune. The Whistler was here. The Whistler was to take them aboard *The Planter*. As they scrambled into their clothes and rolled up their bedding he told them they would have to wait for breakfast until they were on board. First they were to go to the tollbooth.

'Why, Mister Farquharson? Are we to be locked up?'

The Whistler laughed. 'You'll see, laddie. Have you never heard of "the Maiden"? Bad boys who run off, and get their big brothers to come and make trouble, should be very careful of her.'

Peter had no idea what he was talking about, nor what made him laugh so, but the other boys did, and when the Whistler left the room, one of them, a lad named George McBryde, caught Peter a great thump across the neck.

'I'm not going to the tollbooth by cause of you, Peter Williamson. Yon's a guillotine he's on about. They call it "the Maiden", and I'm not staying near you, not even to look at the thing.'

'It's you that ran off, not me.'

'It's you that caused all the trouble! Now give me a leg up, and mind you keep quiet about my whereabouts, or I swear I'll cut your head off myself.'

McBryde hid himself up in the couples, among the rafters of the attic room. There was hardly space for a bird up there and Peter was sure he would die, crammed into that dusty space between the roof timbers, but they left him there and went down to join the others. No-one gave him away, but he was soon missed and his hiding place found; then, with a great deal of grumbling and cursing about wasted time, they were taken off to the tollbooth.

There they were joined by those who had been lodged in the poorhouse and ... 'since it was a long way to the harbour at Tory, and because certain young boys called for their daddies to get them all into trouble,' ... they were handcuffed! There was always the excuse that there were real convicts among them. They, however, were brought from the cells, pale and with shambling footsteps, and already had the 'Bracelets' on. But Peter and the others had to stretch out their hands while the double iron rings were snapped round their wrists and locked into place.

For once everyone had gone very quiet. With their joined hands weighted down almost to their knees in front, they began to move like criminals. The procession that left the tollbooth in double file shuffled and stumbled its way through the early morning streets in misery. There was no piper to raise their spirits, no bravely drumming Jamie to stride ahead of them. It was cold and there were few people about at that hour of the morning so early in the year.

All through the top part of town and through back streets to the bridge over the Denn Burn which separated Aberdeen from Tory they marched in double file. It was still cold, for, though the sun was up, you could not see it for the mist that blew about in ragged, wet clouds, smelling of the sea. Peter kept his eyes down most of the way. At one time he would have been looking about, hoping to see someone he knew, hoping that he could get a message to his family, hoping that he would be recognized and rescued. Walking like this, chained like a felon, he hoped that no-one would see him. When they got near the harbour, however, everyone began to raise their heads, asking which was *The Planter* and trying to pick out likely looking ships among the crowded vessels huddled against the sandbanks and wooden quays of Tory.

The supply boat that was waiting to row them out could not take them all at once. Peter stood on shore waiting for the boat's return. He could see *The Planter* now, her mastheads hidden from time to time by the mist. She was a rather old-fashioned, deep-bellied merchantman, about seventy or eighty feet long, with three masts. Peter knew very little about ships, but even he could tell that she was not built for speed or beauty. She was painted in brown and black and lay, heeled over slightly, against one of the scrubby spits of land that divided up the harbour. It looked as though she was having some work done to her because there was new timber against her sides.

The Whistler and Mr Jeffrey had gone over with the first boat, so Peter timidly edged nearer to where James Robertson was standing, so as to hear what he was saying to some of the men from the jail.

'Oh no, she's not new. Captain Ragg fetched her up from London a short while ago and she's being re-fitted ... The owners now? There'd be about eight shareholders ... Oh, I doubt Captain Ragg will have a share. He'll most like be taking a fee ... From Bristol, I suppose, or Southampton. Not from Aberdeen ... I hear she's been many times across the Atlantic, so she should know her way by now ... It's a new venture for the gentlemen, sending to fetch tobacco by themselves.'

By now Peter knew better than to open his mouth, or to ask any of the questions that crowded his mind. Robertson had changed from talking about tobacco to smoking it and was generously passing his long clay pipe from one to another, although, with the manacles still weighing the prisoners down, it was a clumsy business all round. Peter turned away to watch the supply boat, which had left the side of the ship and was moving slowly towards them. He did not notice anyone coming along the strand, until he was caught a thump across the back, and there was Stookie laughing beside him!

'Stookie! Where did you spring from?'

'They fetched me back again. You're no so easily rid of me.'

'But, how? Your father had the money and papers!'

'They must want me very badly! They followed, until there was nobody by to hear and then they threatened my father with violence if he did not let me go!'

'But that's terrible! What did you do?'

'Peter, I know it sounds strange, and you're not to tell a soul, but I believe I'm fated to go. I want to go. They knew I wanted to go. My father should never have tried to buy me back.'

'But they shouldn't have threatened him!'

'No, I ken that. It was frightening. He could never stand up to those fellows; he'd have been killed. So I said I'd rather go and please would he leave me be, and I'd try to return a gentleman, and a wealthy one.'

'And he let you?'

'He had to. I ran down the road, so they had to leave him to catch up with me.'

'Stookie, I'm sorry about your family, but I am glad you're back. Let's hope we can stay together. Jamie's gone ahead.'

'Oh aye, I heard he was not to be bought off. His father's not a rich man.'

'Did you know that he was taken twice as well?'

'I heard something. Was that what his father meant? They took him from his bed?'

'Yes. He calls out in his sleep sometimes, did you know? He yells out and struggles, as if someone were snatching him up, and then he wets himself, and cries for shame. It's not right, Stookie. Like Jamie's father says, it's kidnapping ... or trepanning – that's what he called it. It can't be right. It must be against the law, and when we come back rich gentlemen, we'll make sure it can never happen again!'

Chapter 10

During the weeks that followed, Peter came to know *The Planter* inside out. At first they were made to feel very unwelcome. This was especially true of Peter, who was blamed for the whole affair of the breakout over the wall and alerting his father to come for him. After a while, however, the carpenters and fitters who were working on the ship found that they could use the extra labour provided by the boys, and more especially by the men. The carpenter Peter had spoken to in the barn helped to fit bunks between the low decks in the fore-part of the ship; and even the younger lads were allowed on deck, although always under guard, and were taught how to splice and whip rope ends and encouraged to clean, polish and grease everything within sight, against rusting in the sea air.

The convicts grew healthier away from the jail, and although everyone spent a deal of time shut away in airless, dark cubby-holes between decks, cramped and stinking from the ballast, they were no longer chained, and their guards were men like James Robertson or the ship's carpenter. They were rough men, but, because they were paid extra for minding the 'servants', they were anxious to see that no harm came to them; of course, they were also careful to see that none got away. One bright day when the pale spring sun broke itself in pieces on the water, some of the indented boys took the ship's boat to go across the harbour and have a scramble over the sands on the far side. But since not one of them could handle a boat, they nearly capsized and were in danger of drowning.

That was the only time Peter saw the man he most hated in all the world – the little man with nervous hands and wiry, red hair – Dod Lunen, who had tricked and mocked him into signing away his liberty. It seemed that Lunen still managed everything: he was told the moment there was trouble and it was certain that he knew at once when there was any close enquiry from relatives about those on board, since a message would come from Dod, 'Everyone below!' and, whatever they were doing, they would be hustled off the decks and kept out of sight. After the episode with the rowing boat Lunen saw that security was a good deal stricter.

Helen Law and her hay boxes were ferried out to them every day. There was a brick-built galley, low down in the ship, just in front of the mainmast, where a huge pot hung over an open range, but this was never used while they were in harbour. All the cooking was done by Mrs Law, and she and her two sons brought 'the diet' out to *The Planter* in the supply boat.

As the days grew longer and the work on the ship was nearly done, sailmakers came out to fit new sails. Peter was amazed at the size and weight of these enormous acres of canvas. He had already learned to scramble about the complicated rigging, being sworn at by the riggers as they checked the yards and lines and fitted new ones. He had learned, too, to scramble around the outside of the vessel while rushes were burnt to loosen the barnacles on her belly as she lay on the sand. Now she was righted and they began to fit the sails. They were white and cream and grey strips, joined and seamed, and as the wind caught and filled them in turn, the vessel pulled at her moorings, and all the men and boys, watching from the deck, cheered and danced to the slap and thrum of rope and canvas.

When she was fully rigged, the pilot took her over the bar on a full Spring Tide and brought her round to Aberdeen.

The boys were taken off and kept on shore while all this was happening, much to their disappointment, but Helen Law laid on a fine meal, with roast lamb and fresh kale, as a change from salt meat and turnips; and it was at her house that they were re-united with Kirsty. Peter had to admit that he had forgotten all about her, but he was also made to confess that he was glad to see her again. The four friends spent several hours together, before the boys had to leave to go back on board, with the promise that they would be together again on *The Planter* in a very few days.

Those few days stretched out into a couple of weeks. Stores were loaded in barrels, chests and sacks; tubs of growing green plants, and pens of pigs and hens were taken on board. Even a cow was brought up a gangplank, lowing and mourning her calf, to give them milk for the journey; and all the time there was Dorcas, the ship's cat, kept to hunt the rats that infested every cargo vessel. Finally, the crew came on board, led by Mr Ragg, the Captain. He was a thin, round-shouldered man, with a large nose and a prominent Adam's apple that moved up and down as he spoke. Not that he spoke very much; apart from reading prayers in the morning, he gave out his orders through the mouthpiece of Mr Young, the mate, whose voice everybody could hear! Because of his gingery hair and round face, on top of a strong, round body, he was known as 'the gingerbread man' by the young people. They soon learned, however, that his easy-going, gingerbread looks belied his real character. His black, curranty eyes would narrow as he blasphemed, cursed and lashed the seven man crew of the little vessel.

As the crew took over the running of the ship, the boys found themselves treated in a way they'd never been used to before. 'It's like school again,' Peter said to Stookie. 'Bells to get you up, bells to get you to meals, roll-call every meal time, rules and beatings!'

'Oh, it's none so bad. At least you know what the rules are. If you do wrong, you know you've done wrong. If that's like your fine school on the hill, I wouldn't mind it at all. I was only at the lessons a short time myself, and it was the minister's wife was the teacher and she was too soft.'

At last they were joined by the women, whose bunks had been prepared by the carpenter. Peter had tried out a hammock, but although it was very comfortable, the others kept tipping him out, so he had a straw mattress under one of the men's bunks.

After arranging their sleeping quarters as well as they could, the women were told to prepare themselves for a party. There were now forty-seven servants and convicts, men, women and children on board. Two more small boys, brothers, came with the women. They looked much the same age as Peter, but they were both so shy that they seemed unable to say how old they were. They, and their mother, spoke only Erse, but they had a relative with them, a cousin or an aunt – Peter couldn't say which – who had a few words of English and could make herself understood. This brought the numbers up to two more than was originally catered for, but nobody seemed to mind and space was found for them somehow.

'What kind of a party is this?' Peter whispered as he stood with Stookie and Jamie up against the forecastle with the other boys, and the small draggle of convicts. In front of them stood the men, and in the front ranks the women, who had spent all afternoon finishing off clean, new caps and aprons. Everyone had been ordered to wash and spruce themselves up. The boys' hair was not yet long enough to tie back, but the men had black ribbons to fasten their hair in a tail at the nape of the neck. Mr Young had himself lined them all up, and inspected them along with the crew. Now it was their captors' turn to feast on Helen Law's cakes and gingerbread. They were all there: Smith the saddler, the Whistler, Mr Jeffrey, Dod Lunen, and Mr Gray, the shopkeeper who had first taken Jamie to be spirited. There were also the shareholders with their wives and daughters, come to look over their cargo of Plantation slaves.

'We've been hidden well to the back so that no questions can be asked,' muttered Stookie out of the corner of his mouth. They dared do no more than whisper, or their toes were smartly trodden on by one of the men in front. The gentry walked about the well of the ship and up onto the after-deck, where wine was served in the captain's cabin. Instead of a piper, there was a fiddler playing fancy dances with foreign names and the air was filled with the light chatter of the wives and daughters.

Peter could just see, beyond the skirts of the women in front, a tiny, strutting figure who was carrying a small, red book, fat with the number of pages that fluttered in the breeze as the little man turned up one set of figures after another. He also carried a wooden box which he placed carefully on one of the hatch covers and which seemed to be jingling with coins. One by one the men who had guarded or 'inlisted' them, came to be paid off in cash. Mr Smith handed over a sheaf of scraps of paper, which the small man read through and entered in the wee red book before counting out a number of coins into a wash-leather bag. Smith saluted smartly, like a sailor, and left the ship.

Now only the gentry were left on board, and they still had much to admire. As well as the new rigging and sails, they were conducted onto the quay to admire the carved figurehead of *The Planter*. It represented a man in a Quaker hat with a spade over his shoulder, and had been newly brightened for the occasion. The bulging eyes had been picked out in white paint, and the cheeks were round and as red as the lips. The figure gazed fixedly forward from below the bowsprit, as if it couldn't wait to see the Plantations again. There was much interest too in the ship's two guns. Peter had heard one of the crew say that no-one knew how to fire them, but he himself had helped to clean and oil and polish them.

Once the inspection was over, the ladies and gentlemen gathered on the after-deck to hear speeches and prayers for the safe return of *The Planter* with goods a-plenty to swell the city's markets; and then the minister turned to the men and women on the foredeck.

'Good people, you carry with you our best wishes for your future in the colonies overseas. I am certain that you will look back on this moment, the twelfth day of May, seventeen hundred and forty-three, with gratitude for the opportunity that has been given to you. Most of you are young and vigorous, many have reason to regret a past life of misery and degradation, but you are all Christian souls and about to begin a new life, in a Land of Plenty. May God go with you.'

With this the ladies clapped their mittened hands, the gentlemen cheered, and they all left the ship for their homes on shore.

Peter had thought that they would sail the following morning, but it seemed that they were to slip out on the evening tide that very day. The people on board held tightly to the rail, and many of them ran up to the after-deck to squint back along the rays of the sun to see the last of Aberdeen, as *The Planter* made her way sluggishly, and with difficulty, out to sea.

With all her sails set, the upper deck seemed impossibly crowded. Peter had never been on a sailing ship, underway. Few of the passengers had done more than take a fishing trip, or a quick, bucketing run a short distance up the coast. He stood beside Kirsty, gazing, like the figurehead, straight out over the bows and the rainbow waves that creamed towards the little ship in the sunset, turning over, white and heavy as she sliced her way through the water.

*

'But you did not look back? Not once? Were you not still grieving for your family?'

54

'Of a surety. But they had not been able to find me and it was too late to grieve now. I had been taken, a young lad that nobody believed was young, and I had to grow old in the way of the world. I set myself to learn. I made myself believe that I would come back home one day, although everyone said the opposite. I thought I would learn all about sailing and, when I was a grown man, I would find a ship heading for home and sail with her. I even named myself Peter the Navigator!

'Were you not sick? Even as a child? You'd never been on the sea before, had you?'

'Oh, I felt sick, but I was not going to admit it. I had to pretend, you see, that I understood the sea and all its ways. When the others took to their beds, I kept above, and since no-one took the least note of a green-faced boy staring at the green waves, I could watch the coast slip by in peace and get the feel of the ship, just as the sailors did. They needed to learn her ways too. She was in no hurry; she gave them time to make her acquaintance. They gentled and tamed her as if she was a wild horse, constantly adjusting and altering the set of her rig. The creamy new sails and hempen lines and sheets were wetted and dried a hundred times, creaking and groaning in every fibre as they found the rhythm of her sailing. And they soon found work for me too, at my old trade, greasing and oiling. I puked on the smell of the grease but I was proud as Punch with the responsibility when Jamie and Stookie and the others finally made their way aboveboard to join me!'

*

It was good to have the companionship of the others, to joke and laugh and sit in the sun; to enjoy the tight saltiness of his skin and the smell of the ship. He did not tell them his plan, but, in order to explain his new-found interest, he said he might be a sailor one day.

'I wish I knew how sailors find the way. I'd like to know where we are and where we're going.'

'Follow the birds,' said Jamie sliding to a sitting position on the deck, gat legged, his thighs spread wide to balance himself. 'Birds and fish don't get spirited. They always know the way.'

Peter and Stookie laughed, and rolled into a companionable heap beside Jamie, on the bleached wood of the deck.

Peter soon found that there was not a single map or chart on board *The Planter*. How could he learn to navigate without any of the maps he had studied on the walls of his classroom? One day, when there was nothing to be seen but grey mist and grey sky all around, he braved the gingerbread figure of the Mate as he sat on the foredeck, smoking.

'How do you know where to go?'

'Follow the birds,' was the mate's surprising answer.

'That's what Jamie said! Tell me the truth, Mr Young. There's no a bird to be seen. How can you tell?'

'There's nothing too difficult, ye ken. We'll lie close till the mist clears and when we see the Shetland Isles we'll turn to the West. If we keep sailing by the sun we should never be out of sight of land for more than a day or two at the most. If we see birds in the air or on the water, we know there's land nearby. There's the Faroes, Iceland, Greenland, Newfoundland and New Scotland. Then, all the way down the coast of the New World until we come to Vir-ginny. Now clear off and leave me in peace.'

It sounded simple, but the reality of the voyage was very different. Day after day the ship crept against the tides and currents of the sea that swept up from the south-west against her. Day after day the sailors on watch took soundings, and strained their eyes against the danger of rocks and ice and the spurs of grey islands that might have been great continents for all they knew. Day after day they shifted the heavy, wet canvas to make the most use of the winds that ever and always threatened to push them inshore, a certain wreck against the unknown, black coastlines.

Peter also learned that sailors, in truth, not only followed the birds and the fish, but also that they could tell from the sound of the sea and the appearance of the waves and the weeds that floated by whether there was land in the offing.

The days stretched into weeks. Storm and mist and unbelievable sunshine. Days when they were herded into the cramped space below deck and the hatches were fastened above them. Days when no-one had time to prepare hot food or think of anything but keeping a firm hold to avoid being battered to death as the vessel plunged and shuddered in the high seas.

They buried one of the servants one morning. The auntie of the two small boys struck her head during a squall and, for all that anyone could do, she lay with her eyes closed and her breath snoring between her greyish lips until she died. The sailors gave the women some canvas; they sewed her body in this heavy shroud and, with some evil-smelling stones from the ballast, sent her to the bottom. The boys' mother prayed and keened over the body of her sister in the wild-sounding Erse that they spoke together, and Captain Ragg read from his prayer book the fine words of the burial service and she was gone. The very next day they sighted the fishing boats south of Newfoundland, and for the first time in many weeks they could be sure of their location.

For a while they stayed with the fishing boats, exchanging news and picking up a few fresh supplies, but soon *The Planter* turned away and began to make her way towards the coastline of America.

The longing to catch sight of land was so great that everyone became unofficial lookouts. The crew were nervous of the number of banks and islands that the fishermen had told them lay around Nova Scotia, so, although there was strong urging upon Captain Ragg to sail inshore and even allow them time to put to land and get fresh food, he set a course much further south and steered his ship due west.

In spite of the certainty that the voyage was almost over and that they were within reach of a new land and a new life, everyone on board became strangely lazy and unable to work. Mr Young ordered sails to be set fore and aft, as well as the usual square rig, to get the most movement out of the ship, but the weather was hot and heavy and the sea seemed thick and oily. Every night there were thunderstorms, but the lightning that played around the masts brought only thunder and very little relief from oppression. Complaint and ill-ease was rife, especially about food. They were not starved but there was little except salt meat, biscuit and porridge, which in that weather was impossible to eat; the cow had dried up and they had already killed and eaten her; they had not had enough to barter with the fishermen for more than fresh water, which had not stayed fresh; the baby had had to be weaned, and grizzled and whimpered itself into hot and restless sleeps and the women scolded and squabbled for shade from the searing heat that drew the pitch out of the deck. The boys hung from the rigging, trying for a sight of land, but Captain Ragg kept to his cabin, issuing embarrassed orders to Mr Young and keeping well away from the others.

Any attempt to draw the Mate into some idea of how long it would be before they reached civilization, or of the reasoning behind this change from coastal sailing to compass reading, brought only incomprehensible jargon about the fortieth parallel, or a terse, 'Keep a look out. We'll strike land soon enough!'

Chapter 11

They were soon to find out how prophetic that was! During the night the storm broke and, instead of labouring under every stitch of canvas she possessed, *The Planter* now ploughed the waves under bare poles. Her crew, sick and scurvy as they were, manned her through the storm, while the servants cowered under closed hatches. With the dawn the storm abated and Peter and the others fell asleep.

They did not sleep for long. A shock that threw them from their beds ran through the ship. Those who, like Peter, slept against the side found themselves struggling in several inches of water within seconds. Timber was falling all about them, men and women screaming, and the ship jarred to a grinding, shuddering stop.

'We've been wrecked!'

'She's stove in! Her sides are stove in!'

'We'll all be drowned!'

'Oh God! Oh Christ! Don't let us drown!'

There was a dreadful, suffocating panic in the hold when they realized that not only were they wrecked but they were battened in. The crew had fastened down the hatches, as they had fastened every moveable thing during the storm, and they were trapped. There was a rush to the stairs. The young people were pushed aside and found themselves standing ankle deep in the salt water that slopped around their living quarters.

'What's happened?' Stookie seemed dazed and still half in dreams, burrowing his way into his breeches.

'Are we going to drown?' Peter was plucking at the sodden bedding that entangled his feet. 'Water's still coming in.'

'Sandy water!' shouted Jamie, floundering about half naked, as he searched for his precious shoes. 'No waves!'

'Jamie! You're right. Look, you two! There's sand coming in. We're aground! We've found land sooner than we expected!'

The Planter was rapidly settling onto a bank of sand and, as she settled, so her timbers were being crushed inwards by the weight of water and shingle.

'Come on! Save what you can!' urged Stookie, holding up one of Jamie's shoes. 'We'll have to get out of here.'

So much was happening all at once, that it was hard to say at what precise moment the people below realized that the crew were leaving. Someone called for silence and everyone stopped battering at the hatch covers or thrusting themselves up the steps. In the awful silence, they could hear Mr Young's voice bellowing orders, the scraping run of the longboat sliding into the sea, oars fitted into the pintles, men jumping into the water and being pulled onto the boat and the thin voice of Captain Ragg: 'Pull for the shore, boys, long and steady.'

'By Jesus, they've abandoned us!'

'Let me out! We'll die down here!'

'Break through into the women's quarters. Their hatch opens easier.'

'If ever I catch up with that Captain Ragg, I'll make a rag of him, so help me!'

'Aid me to find my tools. I'll soon have us out!'

True to his word the carpenter's toolbag supplied enough in the way of hammers, mallets, chisels and adzes to make a way through both the hatch and the bulkhead into the women's quarters. They were more fortunate than the men. Only a little water had found entry and, after the initial panic and noisy reunion with the menfolk, they busied themselves with collecting blankets, clothes and food, ready for whatever the day should bring.

The water in the hold had stopped rising. The vessel seemed to be firmly held in the sand and, after an hour or so of chipping and sawing, the bedraggled little party was able to gather on deck and look about them.

'What's to do?'

'Will she break up?'

'Is this land, or only a shoal?'

'Should we stay on the ship?'

Nobody seemed able to take command or make decisions. Some advocated making a raft, some repairing the ship; all were afraid that the sea would cover the sand and set them awash.

'Let me down and I'll have a look,' said Peter and, since nobody seemed to care either way, he and Stookie got some of the other boys to lower them on a rope into the water, which was not more than a couple of feet deep at the forward end of the ship. They half waded, half swam away from *The Planter* in the direction that the sandbank seemed to be lying. They found no higher point but, as the sun grew stronger they could make out the extent of the bank. The water was warm over the sand and in places only a few inches deep. The tide must have been going out as they struck; nevertheless, there was no dry land, no hope that the sea would uncover any causeway or place where they could walk to safety. The sandbank was about half a mile in extent, but it seemed as though they were not going to be able to get off the ship by any other means than a boat of some kind.

They were willingly hauled on board again. While they had been gone a lookout on the mainmast had seen land about three-quarters of a mile away, and had also seen the longboat rounding a headland some two or three miles to the south-west. The decision was quickly made that some twelve or so volunteers would try to get help by poling themselves over the sandbank and then floating ashore on a raft that they were fashioning out of spars, empty barrels and the remaining hatch covers. The attempt to repair *The Planter* was soon given up. None of the men had the skill and their best efforts would never have got the old ship to float again. They had shored tarpaulins and loose timbers against the holes and hoped it would be enough to prevent the damage getting worse. At least she might hold together long enough to get the whole party ferried ashore.

Alongside all this activity there was a considerable amount of looting.

'The captain abandoned ship, so we're entitled to salvage. That's the law, that is.'

'Oh, aye. Trust you to know the law, Archie Brown, since you fall foul of it so often!'

'Haud your whisht!' said Archie, laughing. 'We're all in the same boat just now. I'm all for seeing what Captain Ragg keeps in that cabin of his!'

There was enough wine and spirits to furnish everyone with a sip, to ward off the effects of cold water and to christen their new, crazy vessel, as it was lowered over the side and half towed, half dragged across the bank and finally shoved off towards the distant shore. They lost sight of her more than once and there were cries and tears when they thought she had capsized, but it was not long before they could see the fire that had been promised as a signal of safe landing. Cheers and yells rang across the water and they returned to the task of preparing for the next high tide.

Several of the prisoners had neatly burgled the ship's stores. No-one knew, or cared, how much went into their own pockets, but a steadily growing pile of supplies was assembled for the next trip to dry land.

'Suppose they don't come back. Suppose it takes ten men to paddle – there wouldn't be room for us!'

The belief that those who wished to be saved must save themselves grew swiftly among the passengers. Several more rafts were constructed now that they had more, and more useful, tools. The timbers of the cow's shed, spars and planking ripped from the vessel herself, bunks, seachests, even the tables from the crew's quarters, served to build floating platforms that sufficed to cover the distance from the sandbank to the shore. The strange flotilla of rafts, canvas-covered coracles, tub boats and floating timbers was ferried over, with the strongest swimmers at their sides, roped together in case of off-shore currents. They joined the others in safety, finding, as they suspected, that it had proved impossible to relaunch their raft from the soft sand of the shore.

Peter looked round at the bedraggled group of men, women and children that huddled round the fire and wondered how they would survive. The land was low-lying: sandbanks, coarse grass and the sea-worn carcasses of dead trees. They could not know if it was an island or part of the mainland. There was no fresh water and no shelter. They had, every one, been soaked to the skin, battered, bruised and shaken by their recent experience. It had taken all their poorly nourished strength to get to this place; were they now about to die here?

And then, little by little, as the tide slowly rose upon the shore their spirits rose too. They had been saved from the sea. By their own efforts they had saved themselves; by the efforts of the convicts they had some tubs of cheese, wine and some meal. They had canvas and timber for shelter; they had a fire. Maybe a passing ship would bring them off; maybe on the other side of the dunes there was civilization; maybe help would come in some form or another. They dragged up some salt-whitened firewood that had not suffered too badly from the storm, dug themselves into the sand-dunes and prepared to wait.

*

'Ahoy there, castaways!'

The young people had been scrambling over the sand dunes, hunting for a few late gulls' eggs. From the top they could see a boat skirting the sandbank that was *The Planter*'s resting place and pulling towards them.

'It's the longboat!' shouted Stookie.

'I wonder he dared. The men will kill him if he lands!' Peter began to slither down towards the beach and the fire.

'We've come to take you off.' It was the Mate who was shouting, using cupped hands like a megaphone.

'Is it your conscience that's troubling you? Murderer!'

'It will be the thought of all the money he'll get when they sell us to the Plantations!'

'What about your ship, Mr Mate? Isn't she worth more than us few, poor, miserable slaves?'

Ignoring the gibes hurled at him from shore the mate went on. 'I'm under orders from Captain Ragg. We'll have you taken off as soon as we can get help. Meanwhile, we'll help you with supplies and a couple of the crew will stay to protect you.'

At that moment two sailors brought up muskets from the boat and pointed them straight at the group on the shore.

'Armed arrest! After what we've been through! How dare they? After what they did to us!'

The longboat slid up onto the beach and the armed men leapt on shore. In no time at all the castaways were persuaded, at gunpoint, that this was the only salvation for them. Mr Young spelt it out clearly in a few short sentences.

'Captain Ragg is even now bargaining to have you taken off. You probably know by now that this is an island – an island of sand, grasses and a few sea birds. When *The Planter* breaks up, as she surely will, you'll all starve, unless and until Captain Ragg can find a boat of some size to transport you away.'

63

'And where's our noble Captain just now?'

'Around the headland lies a river with settlements and villages on its banks. That's where he will get help to take you off. For the moment we'll take some of the women with us, where they'll be more comfortable.'

'In their beds, I'll be bound,' muttered someone in the crowd, but the women were taken, and no resistance was offered by anyone. There was little alternative if they were all to survive. All their anger at having been abandoned was turned to a fierce determination to survive.

By the time a sloop finally came to pick them up, they had been camped on that shore for three miserable weeks.

They were carried up the river which they learned was called the Delaware and to a pleasant town of straight streets and wooden houses, 'The Place of Brotherly Love' – Philadelphia. Here, once more, their home was near the quay in a merchant's warehouse, and here they were to stay until it was clear that they had brought no sickness with them, and until they were sold. Advertisements were exhibited offering goods for sale, with sundry indentures, as 'male and female servants, some skilled carpenters, saddlers, hairdressers and the like, all strong and able to work'.

The Planter had been forced to land them far away from the tobacco plantations of Virginia. Here, in Pennsylvania, among vast forests, there were small farms cut into the land along streams and rivers, where the only way to travel any distance was by boat, and where men of many different tongues and traditions had settled, perhaps around a church or meeting house built for their security and as a centre for their community. If such people came to Philadelphia to take on labour, it was not for a yearly wage. Time was measured in life-span terms. *The Planter's* cargo was not to be that easily disposed of, unless new papers were issued with some assessment of what they could do. Peter was under some pressure to lie about his age so that he might be more marketable, but always at the back of his mind lay the idea that one day he would return and challenge the men who had taken him, under the age of consent and against his will, to sell him like a barrel of herring at public auction, so he refused.

It was in William Penn's country that they learned a new song:

Fifty for a negro slave, sixteen for a white,
Negro's yours for ever, his children and his wife, boy,
His children and his wife.

So buy, buy white boy,
You try my white boy,
You drive my white boy,
And see that white boy run.

Chapter 12

Maclaurin stretched and eased himself into a fresh position on the pile of cordage. Peter had gone below to fetch the bowls of hot broth which had been offered them. He felt sleepy, and as though the sickness and the salt wind had scoured him clean of tension and the resentment he had carried against Williamson for the whole enterprise. He was beginning to take pleasure in the sights and smells around him, the business of the ship and the story that he was only half listening to. He had been aware of the same easing of tension in Peter, as if he too had experienced a sea change. The wreck of *The Planter*, the discomfort of the voyage, and the beginnings of a new life in the New World, carried less pain in the telling than the humiliation and frustration of the time in Aberdeen. The old man thought of the legend above the door of Peter's eating house: 'Peter Williamson of the New World'. He was beginning to understand how Peter felt about his growing into manhood. It was a time he wanted to remember, a time he would never forget – a second existence that, were it not for his corrosive hunger for vengeance, he would gladly assume again.

'Did you bide long before they sold ye?'

The broth was beef essence, thin and hot and strong-tasting. Maclaurin felt more alert, even curious about this place he would never visit, except in imagination.

'Aye, quite a while.'

'But you were sold.'

'Oh yes, I was sold. I'd a fancy in my head that I would be put to some merchant as a clerk in a shipping office but, instead, I herded swine.'

'No yellow stockings, then.'

'Man, ye've a rare memory! No, no yellow stockings, no starched cravat. I went barefoot and slept in straw. But my master was good

66

to me and they were fine hogs! Wilson was the name of my master, Hugh Wilson. He had been spirited as well, so I found out, although he was a man of few words. He had come from some god-forsaken place in the north – St Johnstown, I think – and had no been well suited with his servitude. He'd run away once and been punished severely, but in the end he got himself a parcel of land in the back country and started breeding hogs.'

'Had he a family?'

'No, he was a solitary fellow. There's not too many women in the out-counties will marry a runaway servant turned pig-farmer. Convict, slave or servant – you're all sold men and the smell clings to ye, like the smell of pig! But he was good to me: he never beat me but when I was at fault, he kept me to my lessons in the winter, and every evening I'd to read to him from the scriptures. When he died he left me well provided.'

'Was he an old man?'

'Na, na. No such an old grandfayther as yoursen! He died of a snakebite and when the hogs and the land was disposed of I found myself the owner of a horse and saddle, my freedom and a hundred and fifty pound in honest gold! Oh I was a fine and couthy fellow, I can tell you! I rode into Philadelphia, put the money into trust with one of the Quaker merchants, sold the horse and set out to follow my fortune. I was tempted to take ship and sail home to take revenge for my kidnapping, but the time was not ripe.'

'What do you mean?'

'I'm not sure that I knew, myself. It was just a feeling that I'd to do it in some style; that nobody listened to me when I cried kidnap before, so I had to be sure of my position before I could command attention. And I was seventeen years old, with a new suit of clothes, and the world and all before me! I almost believed I could fly! There were black slaves and white slaves and fine women in fancy clothes, any of whom would give me the time of day and call me 'sir'. There were ships a-plenty tied up at the wharves. Why, it was easier to plan on going to London than to plan on going to the opposite shore of the Delaware river. I could go back to Scotland any day, but, once there, I was not likely to find my way to Pennsylvania again. I took off where chance and my fancy led me.

'You did not see any of the others, your friends from *The Planter?*'

'Not one. It never occurred to me to try. That life was past and I knew no way to find them. I knew that Kirsty had been got with child by the mate, Mr Young, on board ship, and was kept back from being sold. I don't know if he was married or if he kept her at all. Jamie I never heard of again, nor Stookie. They had been spirited away, never to be seen the more.'

'What did you do? How did you live?'

'Hardly. It's a hard land... Man, have you ever felt the cold to your stomach and lungs go clear through to your spine? It's as if your blood was freezing in your veins. It snows there for three or four months of the year, and then the summer is so hot and dusty there's not a blade of green, but only dry hay. I took to the rivers and went wherever there was employment.'

'Carrying furs?'

'There's not much gets by you, James Maclaurin! Aye, furs and goods, blankets and skins. I became what they call a voyageur sent out to bring in the beaver and muskrat, although the canny Quakers made it worthwhile for the trappers to come in to the city with their pelts to trade rather than send men into the wilderness to trade with the Indians. Still and all, there was enough traffic and to-and-fro in many of those places for there to be a postal service. Horses carry mail from New Castle to The Falls, from The Falls to Philadelphia. Why you could send a letter all the way to Maryland for ninepence.'

Maclaurin had no idea what, nor where, these places were, but it was clear that Peter counted it an impressive achievement; and so it seemed, for if they needed to make contact with the Crosbies by letter to Edinburgh, the capital city of Scotland, it would no doubt be by anything but a regular mail service, such as existed amongst those wild colonials overseas!

*

He had no recollection of having been asleep, but he opened his eyes onto bare, tossing waves and found himself alone. His dreams were vivid, even when awake, and how much he had heard and how much was his own imagining he had no idea. He thought Peter had told him how they planted Indian corn in squares, five seeds to a square

68

with a fish buried under each seed to make it grow, but he could not think that the snakes were anything but a dream. He hated snakes with a loathing that was almost frenzy, yet he had in his mind vivid images of snakes that could join themselves together if cut in half by a spade, of serpents whose bite could turn a man's blood black and his body to oil in the space of a few hours, of wounded snakes that killed themselves with their own venom, and of pools writhing black with hissing water-snakes. He shuddered as he got to his feet, determined to rid himself of evil recollections, and to try and locate their position on that section of the coast of Scotland that lay clear and sharp to their side as they laboured against the wind.

He found Peter deep in conversation with one of the crew, their heads bent together over a frayed rope-end which seemed of inexplicable interest. Peter waved cheerily to him and shouted across, 'There y'are, Fayther. I wonder the tale of your son's adventures in Americee should send you so fast asleep! I mind you would maunder auld tales to send me to sleep when I was young, but I didna think to be making you sic' a lullaby in the broad light of day.'

Maclaurin snorted, but could think of no rejoinder that did not involve him in the most flagrant of lies about the supposed childhood of his supposed son.

'We're to put in to shelter for a wee while,' Peter went on in the same, loud voice. 'There's a storm brewing, by the look of things, and a small repair to make, so you'll spend at least one night in a bed on dry land.'

'Where will we go?' He could see no sign of habitation, let alone a town or village where they might seek shelter.

'There's a fishing village tucked in behind the headland. You'll see it clear in a moment or two.'

The sailor pointed ahead and James thought that he could make out the spars of two or three small boats, but no sign of a house.

'We'll be tied up in an hour or so, and there'll be somewhere that'll give us a bed and supper till this wind blows itself round a point or two and we can get more leeway on her. Go below now, Father, and get some things together for a night on the town – and for goodness' sakes pit on some breeks, man!'

Maclaurin looked down at his spindly legs, still wrapped around with the blanket. He had quite forgotten that Peter had lifted him straight from bed and that he had stayed wrapped like a parcel all day on a pile of rope. Embarrassed at his dishevelled appearance and with their laughter following him, he stumbled hastily back to his cabin to dress himself and collect his papers.

It was by no means a town that they came to, but James was surprised at the spaciousness of the inn that stood at the centre of the little harbour. From the sea it had been hard to see anything of the place, but once they rounded the rocks and crabbed their way in to tie up alongside the fishing boats it turned out to be a tidy little village, whose twenty or so cottages were strung out around the arms of the bay, with the inn keeping lookout, like a single eye at the centre.

There was nothing to indicate the storm they had expected. Every rock and stunted tree showed clear and still against the steel-grey sky, but as James and Peter sat by the parlour fire, with the crew of the *Lady Grace* and some of the local fishermen, smoke came reeking down the chimney and the innkeeper closed the shutters against the sudden wind. Turning to the two passengers, so obviously different from the sea folk who were his usual customers, he spoke aside to them in a kind of stage whisper.

'It'll be a rough evening, gentlemen. I've no candles to give ye, but if you would care for a taper in your room the guidwife has the fire kindled and in a while you and your father can sup there in peace. The fisher folk are good folk but a thought wild in their ways, ye ken.'

'Thank you kindly.' James stepped in quickly before Peter could shame them with some suggestion of keeping the company of seafaring men. 'A two or three tapers would suit fine, for I've some papers to finish. We'll pay for the light and fire, if you can give us a written reckoning in the morning.'

The supper was worth the waiting and there was a hot toddy to warm their insides and a pan of embers to warm their bed. James was impatient to put down on paper some of the information he was getting from Peter, some of the names and the scanty times and dates of the confused happenings that filled his imaginings. There was too much material, too much that he could not grasp. He was frustrated at the break in their journey but determined that he would make good out of the enforced delay. Peter had his foul little pipe going and was looking longingly at the door. He was clearly drawn to the singing and laughter below, but whereas on shipboard *he* was in charge, here, in this stonewalled chamber, James was his own man again.

'Sit there a while and let me ask you a few things. I have a duty to the Crosbies and I am still unsure what drives you to seek what seems to me like revenge. If the authorities in Aberdeen burnt your book, saying it was lies, we have to prove that what you say about being kidnapped is true – and for that we need evidence that you were under the "age of pupillarity". So we must scratch around for baptism records and records of the sailing dates of *The Planter*. We need to find the people who held you captive, if they are still alive after all these years, and we need evidence of who was responsible for employing them, as well as the names of the owners of the ship. This is fine, this is our task, this we will do. But, man, you were aye content in the brave New World! What drives you to such lengths? I take it you are not a rich man. This could ruin you and ruin the name of my masters as well. You may have convinced that young fool, Andrew, that he has a case can stand before the Lord Ordinary, but you'll have a hard time convincing me!'

Peter did not sit as he was bidden, but took a turn up and down, chewing the stem of his pipe. Suddenly he turned on the old man with a kind of fury that was so unlike his usual bantering tone, or the dramatic way he had of telling a story, that James was completely taken aback and felt that he had lost any of that hard-won authority he had seemed to possess.

'Did you know there was no difference in the slave market between a convict and an educated man? Did you know that a boy or girl could, very like, be bound for a lifetime of servitude, where a man was free after four years? Did you know that there is no likelihood of an indented servant ever seeing his homeland again, for the ships will not easily give passage West to East? The money is now in people out, goods home. Did you know that the government will not issue coin to the colonies so, unless you have furs or tobacco by the hogshead, there is no bargain to be made? You ask what drives me

71

to the law, and I'll tell you . . . It is no longer my case alone that drives me, but the wrong that ignorant and willingly deaf folk in this country are committing against their own countrymen. Did you know that we are fighting a war? No! Most people have forgotten, or simply don't know. Out there they've not forgotten! England is fighting a bloody, endless, hidden war, with treachery and butchery on every side. Oh, I may be seeking revenge for poor Peter Williamson, but there is more than that, so much more than that! My books told the truth of slavery and kidnap, no doubt of it, but they also told the truth of French and Indian cruelty, and the old enmities here at home that are the root of it all.'

There was a long pause. Peter was panting almost as though he had run a long race uphill, and James was shocked into a silence that he did not know how to break. At last he shook his head and smiled at the younger man. He was relieved to see the smile reflected in Peter's face.

'You're a dangerous man to know, Peter.'

'I'm mebbe a dangerous son for an old fella to be sharing a bed with.'

'When I saw yon mumbo-jumbo with the Indian customs, I thought . . .'

'Oh aye, they said you'd crept in to see the show.'

'Well, you'll maybe think me fanciful, but I thought . . . for a wee while I believed you were an Indian, with all the feathers and the songs and the sweet smoke; and yet, at the end, your back was scarred and there was such pain in your story. But on the ship, this very day, you told it like it was a great adventure, a tale for boys; and now, right this minute, you've all the fire of a Puritan Ranter, preaching damnation. So where does it all come together?'

'Together? In me! Over and over in me! And yet it seems that every time I see a way to go forward, I'm thrown back into captivity, tied and prevented from speaking out; forbye even after I got my freedom, I was kidnapped yet again, only this time, by a Delaware raiding party.'

'When you were carrying furs?'

'Och, haud your whisht on the furs! The fine skins go all to fine folk to make their hats! You an' me'll never have more than moleskin or coney to trim our coats! No, but I'd a small parcel of land to my own, some beasts, and the first crops in the barn when the savages came and ruined the lot!'

'How?'

'They killed the beasts and set fire to the buildings.'

'Why did they do that?'

'Forbye it's their nature, and forbye there's people will set them on to such things.'

'What people? Who would do such a thing?'

'All's fair in love and war, father. First the English would pay them for every dead Frenchy and then the French would pay them for every dead Englishman. But the Indians didn't wait to find out what lingo the white folks spoke before they killed them. And most often they could not tell the one language from another, seeing that they spoke their own tongue only. Besides a scalp does not speak – it just has to look right. Blond or redhead, dark or grey, so long as the hair don't look like redskin hair, someone will pay.'

'They cut off their hair?'

'The skin with the hair on it. Just as any farmer'd want sight of some vermin's tail, the soldiers would want to see the scalp before they paid out.'

'But you . . .'

'Oh they didn't scalp me. They weren't after a few miserable roanoak shells or a pannikin of rum for my skin. This was a raid on my land, for meat and grains. So instead of scalping me, they took me for their prisoner.'

There was silence for a while. Peter drew on his pipe and the peat on the fire sent out a little spurt of flame that hissed and died back to white ash again. The dishes had long been cleared and the singing below was slow and sad, the long, slow, Scottish laments of the sea and its heroes.

Chapter 13

The fire was almost out. Peter took off his boots and propped his feet against the pine logs stacked against the snows of winter. He would warm his toes before scrambling into the box bed, since there was no woman lying there tonight. Susan had stayed on with her parents, deeming it safer and more comfortable that their firstborn should arrive in civilized surroundings. He had taken her over the previous day, but had hurried back to feed the stock and tend the cheeses that could not be left one more day unturned. The list of his duties stretched comfortably before him as he scorched his toes ... there was another hole in his stockings ... it would have to wait Susan's return and then ... maybe then she would be too busy to mend his hose, what with the demands of the baby, and all ... his baby, in his house, lying in the cradle he himself had made, clumsily to be sure with no tools but an axe, but he had burned out the log like a tiny canoe and padded it with moss ... the women would be busy with wrappers and blankets; his child would be warm this winter. Come the spring, he or she would lie beneath the trees and take her first steps in the yard outside. He hoped it would be a girl. In this wilderness where the first settlements were hard won from the forest, a girl child was a rare and lovely thing. He would look out a pine chipping tomorrow to carve a doll. Maybe he could make wooden arms that moved. He had seen dolls like that back home in Scotland. He'd sharpen his knife and see what he could do. Perhaps he could use berries to redden the cheeks and mouth. A real doll for his little daughter.

The fire seemed to smell stronger once he took his feet off the log-stack, the smell of burning straw mixed with the pine. He could hear the flames crackle above the gentle, October wind, that stirred the treetops to sound like the soughing of the sea. Fire! That was no hearthstone blaze. That was fire! Without putting his boots on, he snatched up the water bucket and ran outside.

As he flung open the door... Bedlam! The world gone mad! Against the flames of his barn danced wild, devil shapes! Black but naked figures bending and twisting in unholy dance. And then the scream! There was no mistaking that scream. Even without seeing, he knew that his sow's throat was cut. He must have bellowed in anger because, in a moment, the bucket flew from his hand, the dancing stopped and his arms were drawn up behind his back and trussed with leather thongs. He still could not see who or what had attacked him, but there was little doubt that this was an Indian raid.

They had been so safe! William Penn's treaty with the Indians had held, when all others had been broken. Land was there a-plenty for the clearing, and the Delaware were not farmers on any scale, but largely hunters and gatherers. They had even helped the Germans and Dutch, the English and Scots, to slash and burn fields, to cut down trees and plant corn. They had been glad to trade with the white man in furs and deerskin, for knives and iron pots, for roanoak and blue glass beads. What had gone wrong? Who were these wild creatures. What did they gain by burning his maize; burning too his few sheep and his pig? What wanton pleasure was it to them, to destroy his two years' work? Would they now destroy him too?

Without a word, one of the braves slapped his head down, so that he almost fell. A tumpline was placed around his forehead and he was loaded up like an ass. Through the loops of braided leather and on the tortured muscles of his back and arms were piled the fruits of the night's raid. Blood ran over his buttocks and thighs from the smoking, raw meat carved from the carcases of his own beasts. His house was gutted and set on fire, but not before the contents of his wife's kist and their bed had been wrapped around every dancing figure, in mocking finery. His boots were tied by the laces and hung on his back with the rest, so that they hung down against the back of his knees as he walked.

Walked! It was stumbling, tortured agony – thrust from behind and tugged from in front. If he fell, and he often fell, he was kicked and hauled to his feet and the load pressed firm against his arms strapped behind him. The light of his burning barn had dimmed into the night and the forest before the band slowed their jogging pace to an Indian walk, and it was full moonlight overhead when they finally stopped to rest.

There were a dozen braves in the raiding party. Thin to the point of sinew and bone, reeking of bear's grease and untanned deerhide, they were fiercely exultant over their capture and determined to satisfy themselves to the full. All along Peter had told himself that he must hold still and silent if he was to survive. He knew enough of the Indian ways from his time as a *coureur du bois* to realise that if he showed weakness he would die, and die horribly. Whatever they did to him he must stay silent and brave, as any of them would have done to prove manhood. Now would be the moment.

They untied his hands, retying them in front. With the blood of his stock was his own blood, forced under the nails by the tightness of the bonds. The pain of the blood re-circulating through his arms and hands was bad enough, but the game that was to follow was worse. Having lit a fire – small, since they were still within reach of civilization – the warriors took burning brands and held them close enough to his naked body so that the heat scorched and even seared, without blistering the skin. The flames set his hair alight, and with screaming laughter they slapped out the flames with pine branches. Peter gritted his teeth and closed his eyes. Water ran from his body, from his eyes and nose – down his legs in ultimate humiliation – but he made no sound and stood swaying but upright until they called enough. 'Dog' they called him. 'He is a dog. We will keep this one.' And they tied him to a tree and threw him some meat, and laughed as he ate from the earth, kneeling. 'Dog!' they said. 'Good dog.' And then they left him.

Perhaps they never thought he would understand their language. Perhaps they did not worry whether he could or not. A dog needs only to understand a few words of command, kicks and beatings. Peter became their dog and ran behind wherever they went, carrying their loads, led always on a leather strap.

There was no heroism in his actions over the months that followed, only the instinct for self-preservation that kept him alive. The raiding party swept through the back country, burning and looting whenever they came to unguarded shack or farmhouse. Often there was a dog roaming the yard and this was dispatched before the alarm could be raised. The outlying farms of the German settlers were fair and well stocked, neatly harvested against the winter, but the forest grew dark and heavy to the borders of their fields; even as the first snows drifted across the clearings, the raiders burst from the trees and with skill born of long practice they cleared and burnt, tortured and killed, and in minutes were away.

They took other prisoners but kept none. Perhaps Peter could have warned them to remain silent, not to plead or cry for mercy. Perhaps he could have saved a life that way, if he had heroically drawn attention to himself. By holding quiet he saved no-one. But then his advice would, no doubt have been too late, in the wrong tongue, or impossible to follow. Those who, like himself, were loaded with raw meat, made to run barefoot through the forest and humiliated, were killed as soon as they became useless through weakness or despised through crying. Peter stood silent as Jacob Sneyder, his wife and five children were scalped and killed. He ran silently beside their servant who cried so continuously that he was summarily silenced by having his throat cut. He crept back into the shadows as far as his dog-lead would allow as John Adams was buried to the neck in his own fold-yard muck-heap while his wife and four children were killed and his wife's body mutilated. Forgotten and ignored, he was a good dog and still alive. If they remembered to feed him, fine, if not, well enough. If they loaded him he carried the load, if not he ran at their heels until they made camp. Sometimes he was tied to a tree, sometimes he was left by the fire, tied to a log, as they danced or sang or feasted. There was nothing to be gained by trying to escape. He had no idea where he was and no way that he could survive the winter on his own. He made himself a part of their living in order to stay alive.

After a while, the skulking and killing ceased. The Indians seemed to get some message from the weather or the terrain or the length of days away from the rest or the tribe. Whatever the reason, they turned towards the morning sun, away from the outlying farms along the Susquehanna river, and into the Tuscarora and Blue Mountains. Here snow lay in drifts along the bare stone ridges and on the branches of the pines but there were tracks and pathways that caught the occasional sunshine, and creeks where the water was warmer than the land, and here they found passage to the high plateau from which the streams had their beginning, the place the Delaware called the Great Swamp. The snow had been swept away by the wind and the springs were running freely. The tough grass was grey and stringy but among the scrubby birch trees were shelters of branches, some bent into hoops, some assembled into cones and all covered with skins and pine twigs, thatched and layered against the cold. Peter realised that he was seeing what few whites had seen: the tribal meeting place of the Delaware Indians. There may have been other and more important places, but here were assembled one hundred and fifty warriors, their wives and children, and here he was to spend the rest of the winter.

The presence of Peter, almost taken for granted by the twelve braves of the hunting party, caused huge amusement and amazement amongst the others. He was handed over to the women by his accustomed name of 'dog', and as a dog he worked for them. Dogs hauled rough sledges or *travois*, and so did he. Dogs carried loads of wood and the carcasses of deer, and so did he. Dogs crept to the fire for warmth and a few scraps of meat, and so did he. The women never looked at him for one moment as a man, even as a strange or freakish man, and this almost totally dehumanised him. There were times when he began to think himself a dog in very truth and would snap and snarl over a bone in the desperation of his hunger.

The men did no work, apart from brief hunting trips for meat. The spoils of their looting were long dispersed amongst the tribe, and the whole community lived on corn cakes and pemmican. It was talk and bitter argument that occupied the men. As he lay, curled among the ashes, tied by the leather lead he always wore, he learnt to follow the war talk and to catch some glimmerings of understanding. There was much drinking among the warriors, and instead of mocking or despising those who became besides themselves under the influence of the rum, they respected and admired them since they believed their inebriation to be akin to the trance-like other self that was an essential part of their religious belief. This was normally achieved by fasting and isolation, but with alcohol, the braves could very quickly transport themselves into a heightened state where even pain went unnoticed and strange and potent visions might appear. He learnt that their supplies of rum came from both French and English sources and that the Delaware were becoming more subtle in their dealings with the warring nations, playing one off against the other and shifting allegiance as the situation demanded. The old alliances were no longer dependable, since the English, especially the Pennsylvania Quakers, were hardly likely to give arms or build forts for the protection of these unstable allies. Yet these Indians, drunk or sober, argued desperately for some kind of protection against the French. If they were to take the English side then they expected to have the same rights as any English newcomer to the land, and certainly more consideration than the German, Dutch or Scots-Irish, who were not even of the same strange but peaceable ways as the Society of Friends.

Peter found his dog status gave him more kinship to the people who had sacked his farm and stolen his goods. He was bereft and felt himself less of a man without his hatred. The more he heard and understood, the more he suffered. Confused and unsure, survival was the only sustaining factor in his life. If he could survive, there was a chance that he could get back. If he could last the winter, his wife and child might be all unknowing and safe in her parents' home. Come the spring the young men would move out and either he would be left with the women, unguarded and unremarked, or he would be taken dog-like on the journey back through the mountains to the fertile plains of the three rivers. He had no way of telling how long it was since he had been taken, but after the melting of the snow and the return of grass to the hunting ground, after the birth of the young fawns and their rearing, he found himself once more trotting behind the braves as they ran through the forest on trails that only they could follow.

He knew that they must be near the white man's settlements because they began to travel at night and make camp during the day. The men slept, wrapped in their blankets with their feet towards the fire, and Peter's lead was fastened to the foot of one or other of the men so that his slightest movement was detected. He had no knife to cut himself loose, no weapon, no supplies of food; the hair had grown long over his body as well as on his head; he was near naked and filthy, but he was determined to break free. In the event the opportunity to escape almost took him by surprise. The brave to whom he was attached left the circle around the fire to relieve himself and, when he returned, he did not re-tie the lead but rolled himself up in his blanket to sleep. Peter held his breath without knowing that he did, and then, slowly, inch by inch, he eased himself onto his knees, then onto his feet and crept away. He forced himself to go slowly. The blood pounded behind his eyes and his stomach churned but, crouching and tense, he side-stepped to the shelter of the trees.

He gave no thought to his escape; he had no plan, only the knowledge of Indian travel and a determination to get home. At first he set no direction to his flight but was only concerned to put as much distance between himself and the Indians as he could, before they woke and noticed him gone. In fact he had not covered more than a quarter of a mile or so before he heard them crashing and stabbing their way through the trees. Surely they would not risk rousing any field-workers or Pennsylvania woodsmen by making too much noise. He found a hollow tree and squeezed himself into the narrow crack. He inched himself up until his feet were about a yard above the ground and he could look out among the midsummer leaves. It would not be a good hiding place for long. He was cramped and it was difficult to stay perched at that height without any support other than the outward pressure of his limbs against the rotting wood. It was his good fortune, however, that the party was nervous of making themselves heard, that they were tired and fractious in their midday awakening, and that they were not too concerned about his loss anyway. Just one more stray dog, nothing to lose sleep over. Probably dead by next morning.

The hunt withdrew and still Peter stayed, wedged like the witch Sycorax in the lightning-riven oak. Ants crawled over his shoulders, the sun moved round to shine on his face and the flies sucked at his sweat. At last his arms and legs gave way and he dropped to the base of the tree in a heap. There was no chance of resting there, however. If he was to avoid recapture and certain death he had to move now, in daylight. Crawling, stumbling, and barely able to stay on his feet, he aimed for the sun and home.

When he reached some kind of homestead, it was near dark. He could smell cooking and woodsmoke; he could hear water poured for washing into a tub and voices of women and children. For the first time in nine months Peter Williamson sat at the edge of a cornfield and cried. The tears were salt on his sweaty face but the sobs shook his body and he was too weak to stop them. A dog began to bark and he was afraid. He rolled over on to his face and wept into the rich soil of civilisation, knowing that he could not go in.

*

Maclaurin took the plaid Moira had given him and wrapped it tightly around the shoulders of the shivering figure, crouched on the stool before the dying fire. It was late and he did not think it wise to bring the guidwife to fetch fresh peat and thus have her see Peter cry. Now it was his turn to play the nurse. He said never a word but poured the last of the spiced wine into the pewter tankard and pressed it into Peter's hands, cupping his own around the younger man's fingers until the shivers ceased and he could drink. At last Peter looked up into the dark fireplace and spoke, his voice steady and quiet.

'I was a dog. A wild dog. I'd have been shot at, the moment I appeared.'

'So what did you do?'

'I did the impossible. I waited.'

'In the corn-field?'

'At first. The corn was just formed, milky and soft; I ate some and I crept to the byre and found some string. I washed my face the best I could and tied my hair from my face. I'd have tried to find clothes, but all the time the dog was growling and barking and I dared not go near. If he had not been tied he'd have got me, for I was in no state to run. When the wife came out for water in the morn I made sure she saw me gently, sitting by the woodpile, and meaning no harm.'

'But she screamed?'

'Screamed and hollered and fetched a shotgun, and her man, and put the childer inside and shut the door and loosed the dog, and threw her arms round the man so he should not kill me – all in a few minutes.'

'So you were safe?'

'Not so safe as before they came out, for I'd a gun at my head and the hound with his hackles up at the wild Indian smell of me, but they did not shoot and – yes – I was safe.'

'They took you in?'

'Aye. They were good folk.'

'What did they make of your story?'

'At first, nothing, for I never said a word. I just keeled over and lay for dead. I've no idea what they did to get me indoors but I have some idea that they carried me into the barn first, and fed me drop by drop. I don't believe I can have told them much for I found that I could not speak.'

'What? Not a word?'

'No. Maybe I'd lost the words with being silent so long. Maybe I was too sick. It was some weeks before I could even say "thank you" to those good people. All the neighbours from miles around came to gawp and to offer help with the haymaking. John Bell said he'd never got the stacks made so fast, and all because of his Wild Man! When I found the words and my throat could make the sounds again, the stories they had made about me were better than the truth, so I needed to say no more, and as soon as I could walk, I left.'

'Where did you go?'

'I walked a hundred and forty miles into Chester County, where was my father-in-law's house, only to find that I had no wife, no child, no home and no friendship at all. They seemed to blame me somehow for the loss of their daughter, as if by getting her with child and getting myself captured I had caused her death. My land was repossessed and I was on my own again, outcast and with nothing!'

'What did you do? Back to carrying furs?'

'Man, will you lay off the furs! Anyway, it was high summer and no time for fur-trading. Yon taper's almost shent. Will we to bed?'

'I've not touched the papers I promised to do for the morn. I'll make a start while there's still a glimmer left. Can you sleep with the light burning?'

'Oh, fayther, it's a while syne my ain fayther tucked me in with a light to keep off the nightmares. I'll be fine!'

And so he was. The old man took the warming pan from the bed and set it in the hearth and spread out the papers from his satchel, but he could not put his mind to the work. Peter slept, breathing soft and regular. James was certain that he would sleep till morning, without dreams. The story was over for now. He wondered who knew it, besides himself. The good farming people who had taken Peter in did not; the mother of his child had died without knowing; and as for his present, pale wife, whining about 'bad dreams', how much did she know? James doubted that she would want to hear. 'Dog' they had called Peter and doggedly he had held on to the truth, until now. So why had he told his story this night, in such humiliating detail, so different from the version that he enacted in the howff? It seemed to the old man that there were more important questions for him to consider than who should be brought to witness against wrongful arrest, or whether there was a case to answer before Lord Minto. He licked his fingers and stubbed out the last of the taper. The room was filled with the smell of mutton fat and peat. Outside, the wind still rushed in from the sea but in the room upstairs James Maclaurin and Peter Williamson lay, wakeful father and sleeping son, side by side, until morning.

Chapter 14

James, like many an old man was up early. He needed to relieve himself and had a distaste for using the chamber-pot in a room he shared with the man who, even though he slept, was still a stranger to him. He took his shoes in hand and crept out to the back of the inn. There was just enough light to find his way and just enough light to see the draped forms of the captain and crew of the *Lady Grace*. They huddled where they had dropped the night before. It would take the last trump to wake them, but still he sidled out into the cold morning as quiet as a spider, scuttling through the yard to the privy.

The wind had abated from last night's gale and the sun was coming up clear and white over the sea. He took a short step towards the water, but it was cold and he had left his plaid indoors so he only sniffed at the sea air. There were birds somewhere that he could hear calling but could not see. He'd heard them before ... strange bird sounds ... whooping calls, soft in the morning. As he turned back to the inn he saw Peter sitting on the window-ledge, hands cupped round his mouth, whistling and hooting to him.

'It's a fine morning for a walk, Father. Will I come down to you?'

'Get dressed first. It's cold. And bring my plaid, will you?'

They strolled in silence to the end of the village street. Nobody was about and only a solitary cat greeting their ankles gave any sign of life.

'Will we get away this morning, do you think?'

'I've a thought to put to you, Father. Would the law firm of Crosbie and Son stand for the delay if we stopped another day here? It would mebbe take a guinea or two to persuade the captain to invent a little storm damage, but I doubt the crew would raise objections to the delay.'

'With the heads they'll have on waking, nor do I! But why should you want to wait? I thought you were all for hasting in to Aberdeen and raising the wind against the authorities who burnt your book.'

'I should like you to hear the rest of my story. The final chapters aren't written yet; that's for you and me to make happen. But you have heard so much that I have never told anyone else, and I think it only right to clear the decks for action. It'll not take long, and maybe I should have told you before, but the time was not right until now, do you see?'

James looked at the man, as if for the first time. He had taken him for an actor, had been confused and ashamed whenever he had succumbed to the power of his performance; and yet last night they had drawn closer than ever before. Williamson had not withdrawn, as at other times, into joking dismissal of his story, had not broken off abruptly except to sleep, had perhaps laid the dreams to rest and, above all, had allowed James to comfort him. There was nothing much to look at. He was just an ordinary man: medium height, medium build, light brown hair, light brown, rather crooked eyes; nothing remarkable, when you could not see the scars. But he had changed. They had both changed. They had dropped their defences and suspicions of each other and now they could begin to work together for a common aim.

'Oh, I'll put any cost down to expenses. Besides if we hold off awhile the captain will perhaps suggest the delay himself. I think it a good plan and it will surely save time in the end.'

There was smoke trickling out of the tavern chimney, and they found the guidwife had porridge and smoked fish for their breakfast. She suggested that they remained above until the crew and the fishermen had been cleared out of the downstairs room, and took instantly to the suggestion of delay. It put more money into her pockets and was less trouble than trying to sober the men in a hurry. They noticed that the husband was not about and guessed that he too had made a night of it.

Chapter 15

After they had eaten and the fire had been made up, Peter went on with his story. He described, in very matter-of-fact terms, how he had determined both to draw the attention of the Philadelphian governors to what was happening, and to do what he could to put matters right. He had no ties, no land to work, and money in safe keeping in the city, so he went back to town.

The year was 1755 and Peter was twenty-four years old.

'I had an audience with His Excellency, Governor Morris, who heard all that I had to say and made me swear an affidavit to take to the Assembly. But there was some dispute, you ken, between him and this Quaker Assembly and they were by no means keen to put their hand to any action that involved violence, or would maybe involve violence. They listened – oh aye, they listened well – to me and to the Indian Chieftains who were their friends, and who had the words to plead, but there was little support they could offer.'

'What was it the Indians wanted?'

'The same protection we all wanted. Their leaders came to Philadelphia, exchanged gifts, sat with the white men and asked them to act like men. I heard one of them, a sachem, by name of Scaroodaya or Monokathoady, for they all have different names that mean different things. He said it ... "Act like men and be no longer as women, possessing weak measures that render your name despicable. Put the hatchet in your hands, send out a number of your young men together with our warriors. Build strong houses for the protection of our old men, women and children while we are absent in war. Provide weapons, ammunition and provisions. We will soon wipe the tears from your eyes... But we must at the same time solemnly assure you that if you delay any longer to act with us or think to put us off, as usual, with uncertain hopes, you must not expect to see our faces under this roof any more. We must shift for our own safety and leave you to the mercy of our enemies." And there were tears in the old man's eyes. He had great dignity, that old, wise man, and he left the Assembly saying, "We remember the many tokens of your friendship to us, but what shall we do? We cannot stand alone. You will not stand with us."

'They heard him and they heard me. They quizzed me for three hours, then kept me waiting while they thought, and sat silent, and debated. Then they sent for me again and quizzed me for one and a half hours more, and finally they agreed.'

'Agreed to what?'

'Agreed to allow Philadelphia to form a force for the protection of the back counties. They would not, could not use force themselves, but they were finally persuaded that this war, which was not of their making, did nevertheless involve them and their friends. A hundred men marched out of Philadelphia on Christmas Day and were in Bethlehem, a Moravian settlement, on the day of the Holy Innocents. It has a kind of poetry about it, don't you think?'

'And you were in the party?'

'Aye, for sure. We loaded up six waggon-loads of supplies and headed on to the Appalachian Mountains to a place called Kennortonhead. I'll not weary you with the tale of all that we did, but let this one serve for all. Some fifty of us went ahead to see if the place was inhabited. There was a sort of a rough road between high banks, leading to the river. We were beginning to make a crossing when we were fired on by Indians. We flung ourselves into the water and rushed on. They were firing all the time and we only just made it to the town. There was not a soul about. We made for the only sizeable building, which was the church, or meeting house. I've told you about the cold in those winters, have I not? Well, the clothes had froze to our backs in the short run to the town, so we thought it no sacrilege to fire the benches in the kirk and warm ourselves. We had lost twenty-seven men, somewhere in the river or on the road and the Indians were still outside. Oh, they were a determined bunch! They tried to fire the church over and over again to roast us like chickens. We held them off for six hours until all our ball and powder was gone. By then it was dark and the Indians were quiet. They had set fire to some of the houses, but nobody knew if they were still in the neighbourhood or not. There seemed no alternative but to make a break for it and try to get back to the others. In the confusion we lost touch, and I had only five men with me when we came to the river. When we finally made it safe to the farm where Captain Davis and the waggons were two more had gone, frozen to death.'

'What happened?'

'Nothing.'

'What do you mean, nothing?'

'There was nothing to do but wait. We saw no more Indians; we saw no more sun nor moon nor anything except grey, shifting snow. Then, with the festival of the Three Wise Men, General Franklin arrived with reinforcements and we returned to Kennorton-head. If naught else, we thought to bury those of our band who had perished but, in spite of the freezing conditions there was nothing left of our comrades. Wild pigs had eaten all but the bones!'

'Do you tell me that! Horrible! Wild pigs, you say? It's like stepping back into the middle ages. You'll be telling me next that there's wolves and bears and dragons no doubt.'

'I never saw scale nor tail of a dragon, but wolves and bears a-plenty there are, and right down to the houses of the city, in the depths of winter. But it's when I tell of such things that I know people will not believe me, and when I am not believed in such things then all the rest seems so much moonshine. But I was there and I can tell you we built a fort in the place of the old church and called it Fort Allen and we built Fort Norris in Minnefinks and Fort Franklin, and all the people came in for protection and brought in their corn and kept the French and their Indians at bay. All in all, from the time I had my farm burnt, there were thirty-five thousand killed by Indians ... ten thousand from west of Philadelphia! And all because the French and the English were feuding with each other, instead of settling down to living. The wolves and the bears and the weather were enough to contend with, without them stirring up the Indians against us.'

'And it is these tales that you have put in your books?'

'Aye, and how I was wounded – ye can see the mess they made of my hand here – and fought against the French at Oswego, and of how we were so unprepared by means of our masters keeping back supplies that we were quite beaten and I was taken prisoner.'

'Again?'

'Again? Oh, you mean another kidnapping? Aye my liberty was taken again. The French general, le Marquis de Montcalm, promised us the treatment of Prisoners of War and hoped we would soon be exchanged! All very civil and like a gentleman, but the sack of the fort by the French and the Indians was a picture out of the pit! They behaved more like infernal beings, like very devils out of hell, than creatures in human form ... killing, scalping, lopping limbs! We were spared some of the horror, since they marched us prisoners out, with nothing but what we could carry on our backs – does that sound familiar? From Oswego to Montreal, from Montreal to Quebec, wherever there was a cage, they put us in. And we near starved! Everyone too busy fighting to grow food; too busy shipping furs to their masters in Europe to care for prisoners. They asked us if we would work the land. I refused. We were asked if we would take service with the French. I refused. Finally, even before the war was over, since they could scarce spare the little it took to feed us, we were exchanged for French prisoners and, because by now I was on the official tally of the English army, they shipped me back to England, and that is when I began to make my way home.'

'Dancing naked in the street.'

'You've seen me. Was I ever naked?'

'You told your story.'

'Aye and with enough money in my pocket, I'd my story published in York.'

'But you went on singing and dancing.'

'Aye, to attract a crowd and to sell the book. Until I came home.'

'And ran straight into trouble.'

'True enough.'

'A prisoner again. Fined and imprisoned and banished the city. And now you're heading for more grief.'

'Unless you can help me to avoid it.'

'They'll clap ye in the tollbooth once more.

'They've to catch me first.'

'And me. They'll take me too, don't forget. Am I not your father?'

'So, what's to be done?'

'You should not be seen in the town, but I can go where I like.'

'You'll need to tak' tent,'

'I'll do that. As discreet and careful as a cat on the ice.'

'Where'll we start. I'm looking forward to some action at last.'

'Aye, ye've been the victim o'er long, if you ask me. Now's the time to be doing.'

'We could find out what happened to the copies of my book that were not burnt.'

'Aye, we could do that. But cannier than all would be to put them in the wrong. Not just get back what you've lost, but be sure that they have their noses rubbed in it. It's a shame that the case is to be heard in Edinburgh and not in Aberdeen.'

'The way Mr Crosbie puts it, by putting our case before the Court of Sessions everybody will hear of it, especially the lawyers. It'll be on public record, and by winning damages and getting my books back I can publish whatever and wherever I like. There'd be a fine tale to tell then, would there not?'

'Aye, hmhm – but first we've to get clear proof. I love that boy like a father and I'll not see his first big appearance before the law marred by any unpreparedness on our part. So, when you were put into the tollbooth, you recanted. They'll say of your own free will.'

'I was threatened.'

'Prove it.'

'How?'

'Who threatened you?'

'I've told all this to Andrew.'

'So now tell me.'

'An officer hauls me before the magistrates and they tell me I'm to stand trial for calumny, libel and slander, that my books are to be seized and lodged in the clerk's office, and straightway they whisk me off to prison.'

'You say magistrates. More than one?

'Oh, aye ... and the Procurator-Fiscal and the clerk and all the officers and what-all.'

'But you were let out on bail.'

'I sent word to the innkeeper and he came to get me out. It was my own money, d'you see, I pledged for the bail, but he signed for me.'

'And you recanted?'

'Not then. The next day. After they'd found me guilty, fined me and ordered the burning. They had this thing all written out which was to be published in the News Sheets, even in York, where I'd had my book printed. And it was a canting grovelling piece, so I refused to sign, but they said I'd be put back into the tollbooth and even the town serjeant said there was no way for me to get away unless I signed, so I put my name to it and was banished.'

'So, apart from the officers of the court, nobody heard you being threatened?'

'No, unless George heard anything. I told him to send my things on because I'd to be away in less than a quarter of an hour or I'd be back inside. He might help. He's a good honest soul, is George.'

'George?'

'George Mackie, the innkeeper. He was not amongst the crowd in court – he'd an inn to keep – but I went there straight after.'

'Crowd? You said no-one heard you threatened!'

'There were folk in the court right enough. But they were just folk come in out of the cold and to gawp at the poor felons and the fancy quines of the streets. Nobody I kenned anyway. Nobody to see me shame myself in public.'

'You might be glad of them yet, son. Should we visit this George Mackie?'

'We'll bide with him if you like. He'll keep us proud and not give us away.'

'Fine. As well as proving wrongful arrest, we'll try to prove theft of your books by finding out if they still have them, although, it's a three–four years syne. But we must do more than that. We must prove, and prove beyond doubt, that you were telling the truth in your book: that you were taken without your consent, that you were "under the age of pupillarity" and taken on this ship *The Planter*. We'll have to scratch and scramble to find any record of such things after eighteen years, but without someone to back your story ... I'll not let Andrew into court on your word alone.'

'Don't you believe me? Even now?'

'I believe you. Now I believe you, for I've seen more than your theatre performance. More perhaps than you meant me to see. But we're engaged in the law and the law is not the theatre, for all its ritual and public performance. You will have to dig and delve in the muck to find your proof. Did anyone believe you when you were a lad and it was happening to you? Did even one of the other servants believe you? Will anyone stand up in court and swear to your story of twenty years ago? Against your recantation and a bunch of magistrates and the Procurator-Fiscal saying you were mistaken and it was all a youthful fancy?'

'No. No... But there must be someone. There must be records of sailings, records of indentures, people who tried to get their sons back. What about Jamie's father? What about Stookie's? What about the men who held us prisoner? Can't they be forced to tell the truth? Why else are we here if not to find them and make them tell the truth?'

'Whisht now! You'll wake the drunkards downstairs. You know that we are after witnesses. All I'm saying is that you are now "the pursuer" in court, and before you can go on you must produce "pursuer's proof". The authorities have only to say you signed a declaration that it is all a fiction. The onus of proof is on you. We have to be sure, and certain sure, that all you claim about being kidnapped is true, and we have to do it without being found out otherwise you will certainly be put in prison again – legitimately – for breaking the terms of your banishment; and we have to be so sure of our facts and our witnesses that no court in the land can bend them.'

'Let's sober them up and away after the unbreakable truth then, Father, or die in the attempt!'

'Haud your whisht, cockie. I'm too old for your pranks. The morn will do fine. Meanwhile, let's see how many names you can call to mind that we might seek out when we get there.'

At this moment there was a timid knocking on the door of their chamber and the captain of the *Lady Grace* peeped into the room. He was wan and sweating from the indulgence of the night before, but sober and apologetic. Maclaurin sat him in his chair with his back to the window whilst he went to join Peter on the bed.

'I'm that shamed, sirs both, that I'd take it kindly if no mention

92

of last night … only that we … well, sir, if you could say that we were benighted, and kept ashore by the wind and you no sort of a sailor, sir … if asked that is. It is no real lie, sir, but it would be a kindness, for we'll all say the same.'

James smiled and looked at Peter who was grinning like a monkey. The captain took their expression as agreement and stood up, carefully, to shake their hands.

'Before you go, Captain, there's something I'd like to ask you, if you would do me the honour of sitting a moment longer. You are bound for Rostock, I believe? I take it you do not own the *Lady Grace*?'

'No, indeed, sir. She was once part of the Hanseatic fleet, but that is now near dead and finished, so a bunch of traders have shares in her. Why do you ask, Mister Jamieson?'

They were both startled, for they had forgotten the name they had sailed under. James, however, regained his authority.

'My son here, as you may have noticed, has a fancy to the sea-faring life, but as one who owns shares, not sails before the mast, as I believe the expression is. I have some funds and could perhaps fee him to such a share. How would I go about it when I get to Aberdeen?'

Peter was staring at the old man, mouth wide open, but he had the sense to say nothing and bide his time. The captain relaxed, realising that there was no menace in the question nor threat of complaint against him.

'That's the right place to be. Trade is good and ships a-plenty in and out. You'd get a share in a coaler or a meal ship at an easy price for your son to start.'

'I was thinking of something a little more ambitious – fur, perhaps, or tobacco.'

The captain was astonished, for neither of the men before him seemed more than plain folk up from the country.

'You'd be thinking of Amerikee then. That's a long way to go before you see your money back; although, to be fair, the market is good.'

'How would I go about it then?'

'Shares are commonly divided amongst those who know each other, but there might be half shares to be had at the end of the list.'

'There's a list, then?'

'Oh, aye. Them as would own shares come to court and witness the amount of the share and register their ownership and what the expenses are to be. And they all sign, and the captain signs for his share. They call the papers the Birth Brieves, although whyfore I cannot say.'

'And who keeps these brieves?'

'I don't know. They would be lodged with a lawyer, or with the court in Aberdeen, mebbe. All I know is I would not sail without I knew the extent of my commitment in cash ... in case the ship was lost, d'ye ken.'

'Or unco' delayed in freighting a cargo for Rostock, eh Captain? By foul winds, nae doubt!'

'Aye, just so, sir. So, if you'll excuse me, we'll be ready to leave on the next tide.'

'Very well, Captain, and thank you for your advice.'

James turned round at the muffled choking behind him, only to see, as the door closed behind the captain, Peter, rolling on the bed, with the corner of the pillow stuffed in his mouth.

'Dear me, are you ailing, Peter?'

'You old fraud!' gasped the young man with the tears of suppressed laughter rolling down his cheeks. 'One minute you're disproving of aught but the truth, and the next you're dissembling better than any travelling player. Man, ye're a marvel, and I'll go with ye tae the moon and back if you've a mind to it!'

'Na, na. There's all the difference in the world between acting a part to deceive folk or to take their money, and me saying naught but what we'd agreed on long since – that I'm to be your father. We've to get at the truth, haven't we? And this chiell has given me some very important information.'

'What's that then?'

'Were you not paying attention? There are likely to be shareholders other than the captain in this ship of yours; that's one. And the second is that we can almost certainly find out who they were by getting a look at these birth brieves.'

'If we can find them?'

'Oh I'll get a look, somehow. I can find an excuse to talk to the port authorities in Aberdeen. *The Planter* was wrecked, was she not?

So there'll be questions of repayment, no doubt. You said she was from London, I seem to remember, so I'll take the part of a London lawyer's clerk. I've had dealings with many of them in the past. It's not so difficult.'

'What's my part in all this?'

'We'll look for your Auntie first and then ... go home, Peter. Find your folks, get a baptism record, find out what your father and your brother did when they came to look for you. Find out if they went to law anent ye, or caught sight of any signed papers for ye. Can they read?'

'Alexander can read a two–three words, enough to get by, but fayther never had the book learning.'

'Still an' all, they'll have been to the magistrate, mebbe. Get as much as you can Peter; so long as you don't get caught again.'

'I'll be sure of that.'

Chapter 16

When they were back on board the *Lady Grace* and making good progress for the last few miles into the harbour at Tory, they had a stroke of luck that boded well for the future. Peter was leaning on the rail, looking landwards and trying to recall the look of the landscape around his home, when one of the crew, going off watch, came and stood beside him.

After filling their pipes and a few moments drawing in the sweet smoke, this man said, 'You'd do best to leave the tobacco trade to others, you and your dad. There's too much risk. Leave it to the big boys that can afford the loss and the delay. I've been there and I know. All the wealth is coming the other way. We don't have the goods they want and they can't use cash.'

He was a biggish man, grey and solid looking, slow to move and speak and with the manner and accent of the North of England.

'I hope you don't think I'm interfering but the captain said you were asking about trading, and I've had years of experience sailing with cargoes of servants and furniture and such, and bringing back tobacco from the plantations. It's a bad business and a risky one.'

'When did you go?' Peter had an uncomfortable feeling of tightness around his guts. 'Was it long since?'

'Oh, aye. I've been many a time. We were wrecked the once and stranded. Lost the ship and lucky to get back with aught at all.'

'It wasn't a ship called *The Planter* was it? Wrecked off Cape May?'

'*The Planter*? How come you know that ship? Aye, for sure it was. How come you've heard of *The Planter*?'

Before he had time to draw breath, Peter had dragged the burly sailor to the cabin where James was packing and repacking his gear for the umpteenth time and pushed him protesting through the door.

'Just listen to this man, James. Here – sit here, and say again what you just said about the ship that was wrecked.'

The big fellow looked as though he had suddenly been taken to a madhouse but he sat on the edge of the bunk and said, 'I was telling your son here about the time I was wrecked off Cape May and lucky to get back with anything at all in my pocket, and saying it was a big risk plying trade to the Americas.'

'Aye, but what called was yon ship? Did you not say it was *The Planter*?'

'Do you tell me that?' James wedged both his hands between his knees and leant forward, almost breathing over the seated sailor. 'And what was the name of the captain? Can you remember?'

'Of course I can remember. It was Captain Ragg. Robert Ragg. But what is all this? Who are you and why do you want to know? There's no secret about it.'

'Then if there's no secret, you'll not mind if I make a few notes.'

'Notes? What for?'

'I'm an old man and I cannot be expected to remember everything. Now please – it's nothing out of the ordinary. I should very much like to hear more about the shipwreck. As you say, one should take all risks seriously. Cape May ... that's near the Delaware river?'

'Ah, for sure it is that, and we were fairly taken by surprise, never having sailed those waters before. I were on watch but I never see the sandbank. We were further inshore than we should have been by rights.'

'Driven off course by the storm?'

The sailor was slow to respond to Peter's interruption. A life of voyaging around the coastlines of the world was sure to be crowded with sandbanks, storms and tales of becalming and running aground.

'Was there a storm? Could've been. We were well off course.'

'But *The Planter* ran aground? She didn't break up?'

'Oh, she broke up all right. A total wreck. Nothing left at all.'

James and Peter exchanged glances. Then James asked gently, 'Was there nothing saved? Did the owners lose everything?'

'That's why I say it's a risk, do you see? We had to go back and fetch off the servants. We'd but the one boat, so we went and got help and first put them to safety and then sold their indentures in the normal way. So there was something saved, but nothing like the cost of the voyage and no ship to take us home.'

'Did you see the servants sold?'

'Well, sir, I was not at the sale, as I remember it, but I saw them all fetched off after ... driven off more like ... seemed like sheep, they did. And I knows they was sold because I'd to ask Captain Ragg for me wages and he said "after they've been sold", and I got me wages so they must all've been sold. All except the one lass that were kept for the mate.'

'Kirsty! I told you about Kirsty and Mr Young!'

The big man stood up so abruptly he seemed about to founder the ship. 'Eh up! Hold on a minute. I never said his name. What's all this about? You two are never thinking of trading? It's some sort of trick! What're you trying to get me to say?'

'What's your name, sailor?' Maclaurin's voice was calm but firm. He stood himself between the angry sailor and the door. Since there was little enough room in the cabin the three men were almost touching. 'You're a wise and intelligent man, and quite correct in your surmise. We are not considering trading, but there's no harm in what we're asking. Did you get to know any of these servants well enough to recognize one if you saw him today? If you saw him today in this ill-lit cabin, or on deck in broad daylight? Could you put a face to a lad called Peter? Peter Williamson that was on *The Planter* when she was wrecked, and in Philadelphia when they were put to the auction?'

'You mean...? This fella here? You weren't one o' them slaves, wert tha? But none o' them were ever likely to come back, they said. You're never one o' them? Peter Williamson, didst tha' say? I recollect a little chap that ran up the shrouds and down the stays like a monkey ... Williamson... A little lively fellow, quick as a cartload of monkeys. It's never you?'

He was so taken aback that he began to shake Williamson's hand between two great paws, as if he were manning the pumps. Suppressed laughter ... hysteria ... silliness ... had bubbled into bathos. None of the men knew how to make sense of the situation any longer, and yet in a few hours they would be berthed in Tory and the crew and passengers going their separate ways. Maclaurin took charge and, within a few minutes, had the captain's still somewhat sheepish permission to question the sailor, and to use his cabin for the purpose. The sailor's name turned out to be William Wilson, and he, in his turn, was relieved of duty for a while as they lay at anchor in the harbour at Tory. Having exchanged sufficient anecdotes to confirm that not only were they both on board *The Planter* when she went aground but that he remembered Peter, even to the extent of having cut and tarred his hair 'for all he was foul and lousy in his head' as he so elegantly put it, he went on to swear that he remembered Peter as one of the little boys, not more than twelve, and remembered that all the servants were kept below decks, battened down and under guard, in this very harbour all those years before. James got him to put his name to a statement, since it was unlikely that he would be in the country for several months, if not years. James himself witnessed it as a legal deposition for Peter, who also signed. The men parted on a quietly solemn note – so recently met, so soon away.

Father and son came down the gangplank, bonnet and plaid, bag and bedroll, and made quiet passage for the town.

Chapter 17

George Mackie's hostelry was not dignified by any name. A bush hung above the door and the smell of the barrels and casks and brew-tubs that reached the end of the street was sufficient recommendation that here was good company and good drinking. James snuffed and mumbled, but said never a word, clattering his stick on the stones and leaving Peter to take the lead.

'Bide here and I'll spy out the land.'

James took charge of the bundles and, although it was cold and turning dark, he was happy enough to stand against the wall and take his bearings while Peter slid inside.

The buildings were in many ways similar to those he knew in Edinburgh – granite-sombre and tall. But this place had a feel that he did not recognize. It was not the sea, for the Firth brought the damp of sea air to his home often enough. It was the knowledge that this was not the capital city of his homeland. The business of the sea was all around him, and instead of lawyers' talk of trade and banking, money and property, here was the visible dirt of trade. However clean, the streets still carried the marks of wheels and horses, of cranes and loading, of boxes of herring and barrels of strong liquor. Aberdeen's wealth was the wealth that came from the ownership of goods and not the wealth that came from the ownership of papers and inheritance.

Peter appeared and beckoned him in. 'We can have a room at the back. He won't charge us much. He will put it about that we're family, but he'll also let people know why we're here ... some people anyway ... those he can trust. This is a good place, Father, and George is a good friend. Come away ben.'

The room was crowded with tables, settles and smoking drinkers. The level of noise was such that a Jacobite rebellion could have been mooted there and never overheard. Men read the lips of those whose faces obtruded on theirs and ordered replenishment of tankard and wine-glass with hands around the haunches of the serving-girls, as much to bring them close enough to hear as to feel the movement of buttocks under their petticoats.

'The night is young. We'll stow our gear and find a place in the corner. Some of these will away home the now, what with the day's work washed down. We'll have a bite to eat later. It'll be fine.'

And fine it was, after the days at sea and so much story telling, just to sit, warm and surrounded by hubbub that was none of their doing, and be at peace.

*

George Mackie was as good as his word. He was not one of the good-humoured, red and jolly sort of publican; he was a somewhat tall, thin man with a nervous way of keeping on the move, always enquiring after the well-being of his customers as if he needed to be reassured. He called himself, on the board above his door, 'George Mackie, Vintner'. And, to be sure, it was for the quality of his food and drink and not for the geniality of his company that people came to his door. Under the building were huge cellars which ran through to the next building, a meal-house, which he also owned. At that end the cellars were full of the bins in which the meal was stored – some for animal feed, some for porridge – but there was room enough at the best of times for casks of ale and the choicest of French and Rhenish wines, aquavit or highland whisky to be brought through from next door.

After the patrons had abandoned the inn for the night the travellers settled down with their host to discuss strategy. Mackie himself offered to give evidence in court of the way in which Peter had been constrained into recanting and the undue speed of his banishment. James took him quietly and severely through his story until he was satisfied that it would stand examination.

'Well and good,' he said, yawning without pretence. 'I'm an old man, and I need my bed. Peter, my son,' he said, so easily and naturally that nobody noticed nor even raised a smile, 'you must track down your Auntie Mary the morn, so follow me soon to bed ... and without noise, do you hear!' Reaching across to the vintner he grasped

101

his hand and shook it, 'Thank you, Mr Mackie. I feel safe and comfortable in your care. Goodnight.'

In fact, it was Peter who was up and about first the next morning, leaving the old fellow still rolled in feathers and disinclined to budge. It was another cold, clear morning, and he left the house, promising himself a call at the bakehouse for a soft, warm roll of bread and a walk through his schoolday past.

*

It was some time before he was able to slow down, to take breath and to wipe the tears away. They could have been caused by the cold east wind, but it seemed, from the pain in his throat, that they were the embarrassed tears of a boy crying for his childhood that had gone missing. He traversed the city from Blackfriars to Greyfriars, gawping at the newly restored nave of St Nicholas' church, and then, from Gallowgate round the Castle Hill and almost to Futty before he dared retrace his steps and look for his aunt's house. But when he tried to find it he was lost. There were new streets he had never seen before, and the piers and quays of the port side were finished, the marshes drained and busy with fishing boats and tall ships. He hunted along Ship Row and up past the Provost's house but nowhere could he find the row of six tall, stone buildings that had been his home. He turned into a bakehouse and made some enquiries as he ate the bread, warm from the oven. 'No,' the flour-whitened baker told him, the houses were gone and he was fairly sure that he'd heard the lady was dead that he described. 'Dead some years syne, long afore the new building began.'

Sensing the baker's willingness to talk, but without giving his name or any other detail, Peter sat on a meal-kist and listened to the gossip about the town. When prodded into reminiscence about the enlistment of servants the baker became quite excited.

'Oh, aye. It was well known that there were boys taken. There were folks a-plenty, scraping together enough to buy back the indentures of the silly lads that had sold themselves or their friends to those that would spirit them overseas.'

Peter left the baker with instructions that if he knew of anyone with a story to tell to send them to Mackie's. He pretended that he was trying to trace a cousin of his who had gone missing, and whom rumour had it had been inveigled on board some ship called *The Planter*. The baker was sure he could help – especially since he was a good customer of George Mackie and knew him well. Peter suspected that he owed Mackie money for meal and would, therefore, be particularly willing to assist.

It was not the baker, however, that sent Margaret Brown flapping and fluttering into the meal cellar. The door stood open, below stone steps to the street and as Peter came near he saw George waving to him to come down. Mistress Brown was a handsome, stout woman, wrapped against the cold in a variety of shawls. She had laid several over her large lawn neck-kerchief and had tied another over her starched mob cap, so that she looked for all the world like a chequered cottage-loaf. Her voice was clear and loud and she had a tale to tell. It was a tale that no doubt had been retold many a time, and polished and refined in the telling. Her glee at finding a new listener was only to be matched by the gusto with which she attacked George's ale.

Peter asked Mackie if James could be persuaded to come down, and when they were all settled in the dusty, cold, but sunlit, doorway of the cellar she poured out her story.

'I'm no ane marrit wummun, ye ken,' she began, her accent making James wince, 'forbye it's ma ain kin, ma brother an' sister that's a' the folk I care for, an' baith o' them wi' the Saviour aboon. Aye, I'm all alane, more's the pity, but I've my remembrances, an' when I heard it that ye were ane spirrited man, an' newly returnit frae America, I thoucht tae speir gif ye'd kennt ma sister that went wi' Capten Ragg tae the New World. Forbye she was marrit a twa-three times and weel respectit at the end, wi' a hoose the girth o' the Provost's hoose, an' a carriage wi' horses alsweel.'

'What like was her name, Mistress?' Peter had begun to echo her way of talking, until he caught sight of James' mystified expression and realized that he wanted to make notes and was not understanding a word. 'There were several young women that sailed with *The Planter*. I did not know them all by name, but there is a chance... Wait! Brown? Did you say Brown? Your sister was not Kirsty? Christine? I remember her, of course I do. She was my friend! But I never saw her after we were sold. Did you know she...' Suddenly he stopped, afraid of saying what was uppermost in his mind: that Kirsty had been taken by the mate, one of the perquisites of the voyage, and made pregnant by him. 'She was so pretty! So alive! Was her name Kirsty?'

'Kirsty. Aye, ye're the man! Were ye at the wedden?' She turned to George and explained. 'In this place, Philadelphia, that's in a sort of heathen place, full of dissenting Quakers and such-like that they call Pennsylvania, there are no such decent Catholic Churches nor even the Kirk, and she tellt me, for I've had news, ye ken, that she an' this ship-master, by name maister Young, were all but kirkfasted in a barn on the waterfront, but wi' church blessing an' a' legalities. Were ye there, Peter? Did ye see?'

Peter did not know how to answer. She was so eager to hear good news and the truth was so hard for such as her to understand. He mourned for Kirsty as he mourned for all those young and foolish creatures who had set off with such mixed feeling for the New World; but it seemed she had had a good life, in spite of it all. If she had been married, later, and lived well, so much the better. Women, especially beautiful women, as he was sure Kirsty had become, were rare commodities across the ocean. He thought of his own dead Susan and the time they had had to wait till the preacher came that way to marry them. Mistress Brown wanted her sister to have been married in the barn. So he lied.

'She'd a splendid wedding. We were all there, she was given away by the captain and there was such feasting and dancing! You'd have been overjoyed to see it. But did she ever mention me? Did she say anything about how I came to be on the ship?'

'She was aye full of her news. We heard from sailors, and from those that knew her husband ... and then she was twice wed, ye ken, and it was but two year sin we heard she was dead en' my ain brother, James – the soutar that ment your shoon, Mr Mackie, wi' mony anither and was weel respectit here – he sent for power of attorney and we'd to pit ad-ver-tise-ments in the newspapers thereanent and sent over to recover her effects. She was living in a place they call Saint Croix, which is to the North, I hear, and not near where she was first marrit.'

'But, Mistress, have you not heard her tell of how she came to America?' James' question was open and gentle, for it was obvious that this woman had been told nothing but the best of accounts. 'Did she say nothing about the voyage itself?'

'Na, na. It was some time before we heard aught, an then, for she was no' a writer, ye ken, it was all how she did. She was well used, gentlemen, and she'd a fine hoose an' ane bit land in this Saint Croix.'

'It's an island, Saint Croix, in the middle of the great water that divides the French from the English. I have seen the island and it's a fine and bonny land. Your sister will have been happy there.'

'Aye, she was that. They sent us a picture of the place with some of her things, her Bible and such, when she died.'

'You were obviously fond of your sister. Before she sailed, did you say goodbye? Were you sad to see her go? Was she younger or older than you?' James coughed in disapproval of the multiplicity of Peter's questions, but having opened the gate to a different chapter in her rambling tale, Mistress Brown sailed through, all shawls flying.

'They were in a barn here on the shore alsweel. They'd a piper and all sorts and I'd to visit with clothes and knitted things for the journey, and shortbread I took once. And we stayed together for a few days in Tory at the house of ane vintner like yourself, Mr Mackie, an' you've no doubt heard tell o' him … his name is like to Cutts or Coutts or some such, forbye the place is still there. Now what was the name…?

'William Coutts is the man.'

'Aye, for sure … William Coutts in Tory. We said oor fareweel to her there, brother James and I, for she wad gee, an no persuaden'. She were gey young but, God knows, strang hairted for all she's deed an gone, an' masel' the only one left, greeten an' alane in a' the world!' And the shawled figure collapsed in tears, snatching for the corner of her wrap to wipe her eyes, and, be it said, her nose too, for the tears flowed plentifully for her loneliness and spinsterhood. They left her to George who, having plied her with a noggin of brandy, then abandoned her as quickly as he dared to the tender mercies of a passing guidwife.

'You'd best away, Peter,' James urged, 'before the whole city knows you're here. Mackie has a load of grain due from Torphins, held up

105

from getting to the river, and will send for it today. Could you be ready to go along?'

'Where's the hurry? I'll be sure that George did not say who I was, nor any story, other than you are my father. Did he say to Mistress Brown that I was Peter Williamson? No, to be sure he did not – for that woman would have told her story to anybody, stranger or friend for a quaff of brandy and a sit down in the warm.'

'But there'll be others. Someone will put two and two together.'

'I'll go, I'll go! But if others come so fast and with so many stories, what will you do? How will you know whether they're genuine or not?'

'Do you think I'm not able to tell one from the other? I know your story almost as well as you. I've a good memory, and, before you say otherwise, not just good for my age, good by anybody's standards – you said so yourself! I'll do just fine. I'll away to the Town Clerk's, and the Sheriff, and the Sheriff-Depute, and first of all I'll to the harbour, to the customs house or the harbour-master's house and see if I cannot get sight of the birth brieve of *The Planter*. I'll be too busy to take any notice of sea-faring adventurers, they'll have to wait until you come back. How long will it take you to go home?'

'Home? Aye, I'd near forgot it was my home. Man, I'll take a horse, if there's one will carry me American fashion. A meal cart will be too slow. Give me three days at the most and some silver for the journey and I'll be away this very day.'

'No, Peter. I'll not have you make any such promise. You cannot tell your weird that easy. Who knows what you'll find at journey's end. Go today and God go with you and, when your business is done, come fast back again.'

'Well and good. There'll be some sort of ride for me at the livery stables, and I know George will look out for you, old man, and make sure you get into no mischief.'

James took the embrace that the young man gave him without surprise. So far had their relationship altered since their first meeting and his subsequent suspicion and animosity that they were now, in truth, father and son. He straightened his wig and followed Peter to the door to see him off.

*

106

The horse was rangy and thin and Peter waited until he had gone some way outside the town before he pulled him over to a convenient gateway and lengthened the stirrups. He was not a tall man. The quick growth of his early youth had not resulted in adult height, nor very long legs, but he was used to a different way of riding, the legs more stretched and further forward on the beast's ribs. Remounting, and settling himself and the horse to an easy pace, he set off westward, with no very clear idea of how the roads went.

It was not long before he realized that he had not been clever in deciding to set out so late. The short winter's day was already half gone and the sun moving to his left was low and thin above brooding cloud.

'Come on, Jezebel! Jade!' he muttered, regardless of the brute's obvious masculinity. 'We both need a warm bed for the night. There's rain, if not snow, in those clouds, so move your old bones. Methuselah!'

Old bones he may have been, but old wise head he was as well, and striding out along the road that followed along the Dee side, once they came to Banchory the horse hung his head, dug in his hooves and refused to go further. Afraid to be seen belabouring such a tired old animal, Peter acknowledged defeat and man and horse came to rest. The inn was busy with farmers and river boatmen. The roads had been closed for some weeks on account of the weather, and things were only just beginning to move again. Peter thought no danger in asking after his family since there lay only a dozen miles or so between his birthplace and this busy town. He quickly acquired a group of men who, hearing that he had come back from the New World to look up his family and friends, were only too happy to tell him the lean tales and the fat, the poor harvests and the closing of farms, the good crops and the buying of land. They remembered the ganging of men through the fairs, taking the drum and 'listing servants for the plantation'. They could put a name to the best known and most successful: John Burnet or Bonny John, whose ship *The Pleasant Sally* had sailed for Maryland and made him a fortune in tobacco, for all he left the district a few years since, bankrupt, his debts unpaid. They remembered – the old, weathered shepherds and corn merchants – the years of dearth in forty-one and forty-two and the bountiful year of forty-three when there was meal a-plenty and no-one was

107

willing to engage themselves for shortage of food at home. They told him how, in that very year, the 'kidnappers' were out and about, and how the locals used to keep their own children in the house and hide the neighbours' children away that played about their doors, for fear they might be spirited away to the ships and sold into slavery to make up for the lack of willing volunteers. They could tell him nothing of his family, although they minded that there was a James Williamson kept a plough in Hirnley, but could not tell if the family was still there.

Peter spent a confused and restless night, trying to sort out what he remembered from what he had heard, and being driven over and over the same ground, asleep as awake. He knew then why he had not wanted to ride in a cart, back along the very same road.

In the morning there was a thin powdering of snow on the hills and, as his reluctant beast turned away from the river and began to climb the narrower side-road, he was glad of the roughness of the rutted surface, for the wind was biting and the frost made the going slippery. The horse may have been reluctant but the rider began to pick up signals of home – familiar smells, a turn in the road, the outline of an empty barn against the sky – that made him tighten the grip of his thighs, willing the reluctant animal to go on, to go home. Dismounting at last at his own gate he saw the house, still untidy, still with children's scratched playplaces on the stone path, the snow showing whiter among the kale than where the wind had cleared the ground, and still the contented grunt of a well-fed pig at the back.

There was no Jeannie to scold him for being away so long. The face that peered from the window at the sound of his horse, bore no family likeness, and the man in stockinged feet who came to the door was a stranger. There was no welcome either. The man was surly, having the door open to the cold wind, and apart from saying that he had no idea where or who James Williamson was, or any other Williamson for that matter, made no attempt at hospitality and slammed and bolted the door.

Peter remounted quickly, in anger feeling the eyes that stared out of the little window beside the door. Turning the horse into the wind he set him smartly away from the unfriendly place. It was, of course, only the wind that brought the water to his eyes but, nevertheless, he found that he had cleared the village and was at the stone gates of Findrack. The horse snorted with dissatisfaction at being pulled up so abruptly, but this house, this land, was so familiar to Peter that he felt he had to go through. Tenant workers for ever came and went, their tied houses passed to strangers at the next year's fair, but the landowning farmers stayed where they were, generation after generation. Names such as Fraser of Findrack went with the land and stayed with the land. Would there be someone who would recollect his father? Was there a chance that Alexander now worked for a Fraser as well? Did Jeannie do as his mother had done before, going to the kitchen door to help out when times were busy? He had to find out.

There was a scrubby boy outside the stable yard who, for sixpence, promised to keep the horse in the warm. Peter took a deep breath and went round to the front. It seemed wrong, somehow. As a boy he had always stood waiting, scrubbed and with some basket or sacking bundle, at the back door, from which he would be offered bread and jam or cake 'to eat outside because of the crumbs'. He had never been inside and certainly never been through the front door. The house was a good deal smaller than he remembered – a well-established farmhouse, the door set in a porch with an iron bell-pull beside it. He could hear the clangour of the bell. It sounded loud – too loud! He should not have been so rough with it. A slippered shuffle prevented him from running away in panic and the door was thrown open wide by an elderly man with the most hairy face Peter had ever seen. Never, even in the wilderness of America where men wore their hair long and their beards long, had he seen such whiskers.

'Well?'

'Good day ... Mr Fraser?'

'Aye. What gars ye look at me like that?'

'I beg your pardon, sir. Are you...? I'm making enquiries... My name is Williamson, sir, Peter Williamson, son of James Williamson, that held a plough from you, sir ... or maybe from one of your kin...'

'Dinna stand havering on the threshold, man. Away ben and let me bar the door. Williamson, you say? Come away and let's have a look at you.'

109

They went into a room at the side of the hall that was study, tack-room and dog-kennel all in one untidiness. A cream-coloured bitch lay, growling softly, in a box under the table with several indeterminate puppies sucking noisily at her dugs.

'Take a chair, Williamson. It's a raw day. Will I offer you a dram?'

'Thank you, sir. That would be fine. It is kind of you to welcome me, for not all have been so friendly.'

'Been to your old home? Aye ... well, dour he may be but a good worker is Henderson, a good man altogether.'

'You know who I am?'

'Did you not say you were Peter Williamson? And are you not the young scamp that ran off to the New World and caused his father greet?'

'That I did not! I was trepanned and taken by force and sold to be a slave... Did my father greet?'

'Your father died. They said of a broken heart, but I doubt he did that. Here, drink this. I'll have one as well, although daughter Isabel will no doubt complain and harry me for the rest of the day. Aye, he moved away, the poor man, and died soon after. The bairns went to Peter Cromar that married your father's sister at Burnside. I dinna ken whaur the elders went. You'd not expect me to call to mind every one of my worker's childer, would you now? So you're Peter, and not a runaway you say. Made your fortune, eh?'

'No. I'd not say that.'

'Canny, eh? Close. Well, none the worse for that. I call to mind you were no bletherer when you were a lad. What brings you here? Looking for work, no doubt? You'll not find ony of your kin in these parts. Only the childer that went wi' Peter Cromar, and they're working at the mill at Charletown alongside him. They'll scarce remember you. How old are you?'

Peter was beginning to get used to the pace of thinking that caused Fraser to jump from one topic to another without seeming connection. He also realised that it was not necessary to answer this shaggy creature every time since, more often than not, he would answer his own questions as he did now.

'Thirty years past and gone, eh? Married? Of course, a fine fellow like yourself, and bairns I've no doubt. Twenty years since you ran off and broke your father's heart. You'll visit his grave. Will you bide wi' me the night? Isabel will find ye a bed. She'll like fine to hear about all they savages and heathen ways in the plantations. They're all black folks down there, so they say. Slaves and such. But do you tell me you were a slave? What did you do, man? Dye your face black?'

He fell into such bellows of shaking laughter that the tears ran down his face and the dog jumped, barking, to her feet, shedding pups all over the floor. Into the subsequent ruckus came Isabel, quiet, calm and pale, with authority written all over her. She finished tying her apron, gathered the pups, put the dog outside, picked up the empty glasses with a mou of disapproval, and fished her father a handkerchief from the tail pocket of his own shabby coat. In a few seconds order was restored and she stood, hands on hips, turning her gaze from one shamefaced man to the other.

'Shame on you both!' she said, and they hung their heads. 'Father, you'll make yourself ill again.' And she stood quietly, like a school teacher waiting for an explanation.

'This is Peter Williamson, my dear. Him that ran ...'

'That was kidnapped, and sold into slavery!' He was determined to get the whole story straight, before bedlam erupted again or Fraser broke in on him once more. 'I've come to find out something about my family; to get my baptism record if I can; to prove that I was still a schoolboy when I was spirited from the streets of Aberdeen and to find anyone who'll testify that I did not run off, but that I was taken against the wishes of my family. I want your father to help me. I've had a hard life. I did not live richly in America, eating sugar and drinking wine. Those are all fairy stories. I was captured by Indians, tortured and starved ... I'm here to get help. The last time I came, I was put into the tollbooth as a scandalous liar and banished from my homeland. If I'm caught this time it'll be worse still. I've a lawyer to plead my case in the courts in Edinburgh, but I must have proof. Solid proof from people of some standing. Will you help me?'

It was Isabel he was addressing, and it was the woman herself who answered.

'Of a certain we will, won't we, Father? The best thing we can do is to have a gathering of the folk hereabouts. Would you know who to ask, Father?'

'Who to trust, more like! Do you say we must break the law, just to aid a runaway?'

'Sir,' broke in Peter quickly, 'I am no' a runaway, and it's they who have broke the law in unjustly fining and banishing me, stealing my books and burning them. I'm here to uphold the law, not to break it.'

'Books d'you say? Are you a scholar, then?'

'No, but I had written the story of my adventures and I was entertaining the public...'

'What the devil...!'

'Father.'

'I was performing Indian dances to attract attention to my story.'

'Disgraceful! Would you do them again ... if I asked you? Would you entertain some of these rustics you insist I ask to my house? Eh? That would shock the neighbours? What do you say, my dear?'

'You're a wicked old man, and you may well be right. But would it not be dangerous to draw attention to Mister Williamson?'

'What's the harm of a private show in a man's own house? Send the boy and get them here tonight. It'll save me the price of feeding the carlins; I'll not even have to give them drink.'

'Don't be so mean, Father. Give me a list of names and I'll send the lad to summon them.'

'There's just one thing, sir.' Peter was somewhat off balance, but it seemed clear that whatever Fraser said would come to pass. 'I dress up! I put on feathers and warpaint, and ... well, I've nothing but what I stand up in.'

'Nonsense. We've geese and grouse, and I daresay you can use berries or mud or some such to colour your face. Did I not say you painted yourself black?' He began to laugh uproariously again, but Isabel asked quietly for the list of names and the whiskered farmer subsided into chuckles.

*

Francis Fraser of Findrack was as good as his word. Chuckling and rushing from one room to another he found feathers that had been stuck in jars to act as pipecleaners; he found pieces of cloth, blanket and leather; he turned out, from amongst the debris of years that

112

cluttered the rooms, everything that Peter asked for. The two men were as busy as children preparing a play for serious adults. They cleared one of the rooms of furniture, leaving only the fixed settles and some chairs.

'These are not young men, Williamson. You cannot discompose them on the floor. Give them a chair, for God's sake!'

The list of names had included the minister, who was a new man, and Peter Cromar from Burnside, but not Williamson's own brothers, since he had not felt easy about performing before kin. The rest were names that he could recall but not fit faces to, nor where they lived. Would William Wilson come from Cloak, that had been sponsor at his baptism? Fraser was certain that they would all attend his summons, as if he'd sent out the brand to all the clan in some highland battle call. His certainty and enthusiasm, and the speed with which the whole affair was rushing along gave Peter a heightened nervousness. He was cold and sweating, and fear swept up in sudden waves from the depths of his belly to his face, drying his mouth and shaking his voice. God, but he was glad that he did not do this for a living! Once in a while was bad enough, but this performance was the worst of all.

There was none of the atmosphere of his room in Edinburgh. He could not weave the magic for this handful of hard-headed farmers. He concentrated on the street-theatre part of his repertoire: telling the story, making them laugh, shocking and shaming them by the strangeness of it all; then, abruptly, he broke off the performance, dropped into his normal voice, and demanded whether it was right that a mere boy should be snatched from the security of his family home in their midst, on their land, and sent overseas by force, and, after being near drowned, captured and enslaved, should now be prevented from ever returning to that home or holding up his head amongst them as a man of honour in his own country.

It came out as a tirade. He had not meant to be so emphatic. He had intended to be cool and sophisticated. Certainly there was none of the hushed silence that followed his shows in Edinburgh. These men, sitting on the hard chairs at the fire-side burst into talk immediately, and not to him. They turned to each other and buzzed with chat. Peter felt flat and insignificant. He wrapped the blanket round his shoulders and went outside to put on his clothes. Isabel was in the corridor carrying a tray of toddy glasses and a steaming bowl. 'You didn't watch?'

'No. I was making punch. If you wish to put on your breeks, please use the study. There'll be something hot for you too when you are dressed.'

Peter knew he had been put in his place ... the travelling player, tolerated and applauded but never accepted in the front parlour. It was a wonder she had not suggested feeding him in the kitchen.

Once dressed his reception was warmer than he had expected. The men were still talking to each other, but he realized that they were talking about his business. They looked up, all of them glass in hand, and took him in. The minister was first to shake him by the hand and promise him baptismal records and even a copy of his name on the school register that was held at the manse. Mr Wilson of Cloak had come at the summons and now held the floor with a ponderous and poetic style that sat well with his immense build, fine, flowing white hair and somewhat clouded, blue eyes. He admitted to 'about sixty years' and said that he had been perfectly well acquainted with James Williamson in Hirnley but was sorry to tell his son that he had died about thirteen or fourteen years ago. He also took Peter by the hand, but did not shake it. He clasped it in his two huge fists and searched Peter's countenance closely, his whisky breath warm on the younger man's face. Then he turned to the men by the fire, straightened up and spoke, as if giving testimony before the elders.

'I know, and would swear, that this man here before me is the very same identical Peter Williamson whose baptism I attended. He is James Williamson's third son. When he went down towards Aberdeen to go to school he went a-missing and, a search being made for him by his father, they could not find him out; and when he could not find him out his father lamented his loss, and his lamentation was very sore and grievous!' He cleared his throat, let go of Peter's hand and sat back down, upright against the wall.

After that, the others clamoured their stories, although they still avoided addressing Peter directly. These were men who had no sense of days or centuries, and whose calendar had been shaped by the major events in their lives and the life of the land. 'It was before the

114

forty-five,' they would say. 'Two or three years before the battle of Culloden...' or mebbe it would be upwards of four years before the battle of Culloden.' He heard of his father and Alex searching for him, of how his father wept when saying that he was kept under guard in a barn and they could not get near; of how the family moved about the area and finally dispersed; of the yearly fairs and the promises made to those who enlisted as servants that they would be returned in a few years when their service was up; and how nobody ever saw them again; and names ... Bonny John and John Elphinston, and a man called Smith of Aberdeen who was big in the slave-trade, but what name or calling Smith had they could not say.

The flood ran down as the toddy ran dry. The men shifted their feet and thought of the cold walk home. Peter thanked them all. They thanked him; they thanked Fraser. No-one referred to the performance; no-one asked him more about his time in the New World.

'Were they not interested?' he asked, when they were all gone and he and Fraser were putting back the furniture.

'Interested? Yon show of yours will be the conversation of the whole neighbourhood. Whyfore would they not be interested?'

'They asked no questions. They did not look at me until I came back, until John Wilson had given his word for me; even then they told their own sad stories to each other.'

'Put that rug under the table, it does not belong there. You've been away o'er lang! Did you not think, mebbe they were feeling guilty?'

'Guilty? Why so?'

Isabel had come silently into the room. She held in her arms his discarded feathers. 'You showed them scars they could not imagine, and you showed them a savage land they could not understand. They felt guilty because they had known all along that such things happened, that folks were sent away in times of hardship and never came back. They had chosen to believe that life out there was good. If what you showed them was true, then your father cried for you without comfort and died without ease, and they are guilty.'

'But you didn't watch.'

'I saw you when you came out. I have seen your nakedness.'

Her father snorted, but said nothing. Peter reached for the rags and tatters that had been his costume but she threw them on to the fire. The stench of burning cloth and feathers quickly filled the room.

'There's one way out of the bad conscience you've given them,' Fraser said, leading them out. 'They'll all come forward now to make their depositions. You'll have me for a start. I'll stand up before anyone. But now I'm away to my bed. Whatever possessed you to burn that rubbish, daughter? The place will stink for days!'

Isabel made no reply but handed him his candle from the side table in the hall and he huffed his way upstairs to bed.

Chapter 18

James watched Peter to the end of the wynd and then went indoors. Although he had given him leave of absence he did not, in his heart of hearts believe that it would take the young man long. Twenty years, give or take a year, was an age to be away from a place. Who knew what he would find, if anything? Himself, he needed to move swiftly, for there were things that he wanted clear before Peter returned and ran into trouble. He got George to promise that anyone who turned up, as Mistress Brown had done, out of the blue, would be asked to come back later and to leave a name. George himself also promised to ask around. Then the old man wrapped his cloak more tightly around his shoulders and went about his business.

The customs house was crowded with shipmasters and errand boys, and by the time James came to the counter it was only to find that they did not keep the Birth Brieves nor any record of the ownership of *The Planter*. 'Try the Harbour Master's house,' he was told. 'They'll no doubt let ye have sight of it.' And sight of it was all he had. He was not allowed, even in his carefully studied alias as representative of the original London owners of *The Planter*, to take a copy. He made a note of the names on the document, however.

'Tell me, young man,' he said to the pock-marked clerk who hovered above the papers as if afraid he would turn them into dust or set fire to them with his breath, 'who of these gentlemen might I find living, if it was a case of them getting some compensation for the loss of the vessel?'

The boy breathed heavily over the desk and pondered.

'Oh, I know it's a long time ago, but there must be someone who could help me trace these men. After all, even their dependants might qualify. It would help if I could track them down quickly. The law's a slow enough animal, but when it comes to a decision it would be a shame if they lost out for want of speed.'

Still the clerk stared at the papers, immovable, blowing through loose lips. Finally he raised his head and nodded. Then, resuming his stare, with a stubby finger he traced the signatures one by one. James quickly took out his notebook and ticked off the names.

'William Smith, James Black, Alexander Mitchell, John Elphinston, Patrick Barron... He was in here yester e'en ... Walter Cochran, William Fordyce. They all signed as sharers in the vessel. As far as I know they're all alive, mister.'

'And which of these men should I find the first? The one that was here yesterday? Is he someone I could come to easily? Is he hereabouts perhaps?' The slow heaviness of the man was driving him insane. He wanted to get this settled before Peter came back.

'Ye could find him in his workplace. He'll perhaps be working late. He has a two-three bits of furniture bound for overseas and to be loaded in the morning. Aye, he'll no doubt be working late. He'll not want to be disturbed, you understand.'

'I understand, but even a busy man will stop, if there's a chance of profit in the wind. I'll be grateful for the whereabouts of Patrick Barron and I'll wish you good day.'

The directions led him to a neat and well set out cabinet maker's shop near the harbour. Barron *was* working late and seemed frantically unable to answer Maclaurin's questions.

'*The Planter*? Man, that was years ago. And I came late into it, as you might say. I really had nothing to do but send some furniture in her, and, if I remember, I fitted her out. Don't ask me about it. If there's money due, my share will be small enough. A seventh part! ... Be careful with that box! Am I to do everything myself?'

He bustled away to cuff the ears of an apprentice and see to the crating of what seemed to be very beautiful and, no doubt, expensive, pieces, now dismantled into component parts and being packed in shavings, sacking and crates. James stood his ground and waited.

'Are ye still here? What more can I tell you? I think it hard that you trouble me with such things when you can see I'm busy.'

'I'll not take too much of your time I promise. Part of the cargo of *The Planter* was a human one. Indented servants.'

'Well? That was no doubt what I was there for. I was mebbe fitting out the 'tween decks with beds and so on.'

118

'Do you recall it at all? Do any of them come especially to mind?'

'How should I know? I can't recall that I ever saw any servants. Now will you let it be? I'll lose more by delay here than ever the past will pay me.'

'Just one more question, Mister Barron. Do you know any of the other shareholders who might have been responsible for the enlisting of servants?'

'Aye, very like. But I cannot remember now. The captain told me that if I was to ship stuff to America I would do well to take a share, since it would save me freight charges, and so I did, but the servants were already on board. I had nothing to do with servants. And then the wretched ship sunk and there an end. Now if there's compensation other than the wee, small pittance we got from the roup and sale of the servants, I'll take it, but at this moment I have other fish to fry so ... good day to ye!'

James was thrust out of the small wicket set in the large workshop door and he heard the lock turn behind him.

'Go and talk to Walter Cochran. He's the one you should see.'

The voice came muffled by the heavy door and then all he could hear was the hammering and sawing of rough pine as the crates were hastily assembled. Walter Cochran! The name was familiar. Where had he heard it before? He wished he'd been able to read upside down the document that lay on the clerk's desk. Sometimes he had been able to make out detail, significant detail, from such upside down papers, but now his sight was older and the spider hand with so many loops and scrawls had told him nothing. Cochran ... not an unusual name in that part of the world. Why did he immediately think of a small man with a book clasped against his side? Oh well, he'd talk to George Mackie about it. Tomorrow he'd other people to see. The Town Clerk for one.

*

The extent of the underground network of gossip and intrigue that centred itself on George Mackie's establishment should not have surprised Maclaurin, for already he had understood that the Mackies formed a clan as close as any highland family, with all the loyalties and complexity of relationships that that entailed. Certain it was that when he walked in through the door that evening strangers came to him and took him by the hand without greeting, suggesting by their heavy silence a wealth of inside knowledge and understanding. Others put their heads together and, with many glances in his direction, buzzed and hummed with muttered encouragement. George came over and steered him to a place aside.

'Were ye to bespeak a jug or two in this company ye'd have no need to go traipsing the streets, forbye there's tales eneugh in this very chaumer would fill a book of two volumes.'

'Thank you, George. I will certainly take great pleasure in treating the company, and yourself, my friend. But let us not stop at a jug or two. It's a cold night. Could ye not brew us a bowl of something cheering to start us off?'

And so the gates were opened. Maclaurin was surprised to find that among all the men in the room there were several women, and not the women of loose morals that he had supposed they might be, but the wives and mothers of Aberdeen, come with demands for redress against ancient grievances. George, he thought, must have sent runners out to gather this group together, and he blessed him for his energy on Peter's behalf.

George himself, ladling hot toddy into glasses, started the proceedings with a confession, which earned him some friendly jeering. Before James had appeared he must have explained the purpose of the evening's gathering, for he plunged straight in, addressing, not James, but the whole assembly.

'You all know Cousin Hugh! Hugh Mackie, that's not content wi' stabling horses but when Bonny John Burnet comes by some years since, with cash jingling in his pocket, takes to stabling boys alsweel.'

'Ay, the world knows there was more besides hay and straw in his byres. Chief of all when there was freetraders in the neighbourhood.'

'But you and I seed Hugh taking up boys for the Plantations, him and the others that had stables. Wilson and Harry Black all had lads sleeping in the straw.'

George, seeing that the tide was loosened, stationed himself at Maclaurin's elbow and gave the names of the speakers in an undertone so that James could record them in his notebook.

'Those two are George Leslie, works for a mason, and Christian Findlater that was, now his wife...'

'Aye, Hugh Mackie, and a gang of five or six boys along with him, was at the back of Gallowgate, when I was at work in the yard there, and they saw this loon coming down the street and they took hold of him, but the boy struggled and got out of their grips. Weel, Hugh kicked the lad with his foot and turned him into the loch, and hurt him sair and he was put into Harry Black's house for a week or so till he recovered. I dinna ken what became of him after.'

'But the time we both saw them was when we saw Hugh driving a parcel of boys before him down Gallowgate, with a staff in his hand.'

'Aye and chasing boys in at closes, like they were stirks.'

James, looking up from his writing, said, 'Could you say what year this was?'

'Oh,' said Christian, looking from one to another of the company, 'it was some years before the battle of Culloden.' And the company nodded and agreed sadly.

'Aye, it was not like the highland folk leaving the land, forced out by the taxes.'

'No, there's no shortage of men willing to go from the high hills these years gone by.'

'And women and childer too.'

'It's been a cruel time for the country.'

'Depopulation, they call it in England.'

'But *before* Culloden, if you'd to get a whole ship laden with servants ye'd to scour the land.'

James was beginning to feel at home, beginning even to enjoy himself. This was his work; this was his life, and he felt the power returning after so long in mourning. He stood up, carefully laid his writing materials on the table and cleared his throat. There was a silence that was both expectant and awed, and he rather ashamedly enjoyed that too.

'I'd best explain. You will have been used to the baileys and their courts and some of you may know the Sheriff's court...' There was a murmur of laughter and a few sideways glances. James played along with the moment... 'Intimately, mebbe. Well, we think this is not

121

something that is best heard in the Sheriff's court. Both Peter Williamson and the lawyers that represent him are convinced that this whole matter of kidnapping and selling young people into slavery ... never mind what they say about indentures, they're not likely to be free to come home, are they? ... The whole matter of slavery itself and the right to buy and sell people like beasts should be taken to the Court of Session, in Edinburgh. Now, even there, we cannot say that the case is being brought against those people who took your children and sold them. All we have is a case of wrongful arrest against those same baileys, and the Sheriff-Depute. Williamson came back to his homeland after unbelievable adventures and ... well you know the rest... Now all that comes about because, when nobody else could, he dared to return and tell the tale. I have to get depositions for the Lord Ordinary, which will be presented to him, in person, by a lawyer, and which he will also read for himself. Then he will say whether, in his opinion, Peter Williamson was telling the truth, that there was no slander in his story and that he should not be banished nor his book burnt. To do this we need your evidence, in writing, which I will attest, by putting my name to the papers, in sight of you all. It may be that I will need to put your story into legal language, which you all know is full of "heretofores" and other rubbish; and everything you say will be in the third person. Here's what George Leslie's story will read like in court ... George Leslie, page something or other, letter C, depones: That about the year 1742, it was the current report that Hugh Mackie, stabler in Aberdeen, was employed by John Burnet, merchant in Aberdeen, for taking up young boys, that they might be carried to the Plantations; Depones: That the said Hugh Mackie, with a gang of five or six boys along with him, was at the back of the Gallowgate where the deponent was working as a mason's servant ... and so on.'

There was applause and laughter for George Leslie, and the room was full of chat and good nature. They turned to Christian, his wife, as well, laughing and congratulating the two of them. James looked on, contented. It would be an easy matter now to take all that Andrew could possibly need, and more. He sat down again and took up his pen, hardly aware that the door at the back of the smoke-clouded room, had been opened enough to let a man slip out, and closed

122

quietly again. What he did notice was the small commotion that was going on in the centre of the group where an old fellow seemed to want to rise and speak, though it was difficult to be sure whether he was being encouraged or hindered in this endeavour. George Mackie introduced him to James.

'Yon's James Kemp. He's an old man, an' mebbe a bit wandering in his mind, but his tale is as clear as yesterday. Oh, an' by the way, I'd best explain... He's a painter.'

It was as well that he had explained, otherwise James might well have thought himself dreaming, for the man that came shuffling towards him, was green from head to foot. His sparse hair was green, his face was green and, although his working clothes bore traces of other colours spattered over them, green was the predominant colour on these too.

'Can you assist me?' The green man offered James a piece of old blanket. 'Just spread it on yon chair, so's I can sit down.'

James spread it out and the old painter lowered himself onto the spindly seat, facing the audience, with all due attention to the tankard that he nursed in his moss-green mottled hands.

'You're after speirin' wha's had bairns spirited frae their hames, an' no able to get them back? Well I'd the twa boys, baith ta'en, an' I'd the deil to pay to get Peter back, an no sooner done than the ither ups an gangs loose, an awa' e'er I could come by him. Now ye canna chain boys like dogs in the yaird, an I lost the twain o' them to the plantations.'

Although it was likely that everyone in the room that day had been bored to death a thousand times by James Kemp and his story, there was the kind of silence that a clever teacher gets when telling a favourite story to a bunch of unruly children at the end of a long day. Maclaurin was almost afraid to break in, but the painter was looking into his tankard. George held the jug up questioningly and James signed for the tankard to be filled. He used the interruption to speak seriously to the green man.

'Mister Kemp, one moment. Your evidence is very important and I must be sure to get it right. If you were present in the court you would be asked to repeat your story on oath, and the lawyers would be able to ask you questions. Do you mind if I ask you questions, exactly as if you were on oath now?'

123

'I'm no accustomed to lying, nor to having folks doubt my word!'

'I don't doubt your word, Mr Kemp. I just want to put your story clear. It's the way the law behaves, I'm afraid. Question and answer, question and answer. Now, your son's name was Peter Kemp?'

'Aye, the elder.'

'Did he sail on *The Planter* with Captain Ragg?'

'He did that.'

'And he was taken by force?'

'No! Now I never said that. You canna' accuse me o' lying.'

'Mister Kemp, you are the most perfect witness. There's no lawyer on this earth could make you say anything that was not the Gospel truth. Was any persuasion used?'

'No. There was never any undue means of any kind used to seduce or persuade by fair promises, or otherwise, to engage or indent him as a servant.'

'But you said he was spirited.'

'Aye, so he was – but that was after.'

'After what?'

'After I'd run round and around and paid money that I could ill afford to get him back. And I *did* get him back, and I had him in my house again, until yon Captain Ragg comes and threatens me in the street.'

'You're sure it was the captain?'

'Mebbe aye, mebbe no. Who else would it be?'

'I don't know, Mister Kemp. What did this man say when he threatened you?'

'There was others by, and they'd clubs or some such in their hands, but he, this man, said that I'd to send Peter back to the ship, for if I did not they would take care of me.'

'What did you understand he meant by that?'

'He made it quite clear. He said I would find myself in the tollbooth.'

'You are sure of that? In the tollbooth?'

'Aye, I'm only telling you what I know for sure. He said I would be put into the tollbooth.'

'And you don't know who this was?'

'If it was not the captain then I don't know who it was.'

'Do you think a sea-captain has the right to put anyone in the tollbooth?'

'No. I suppose not.'

'Who does have the right?'

'One of the Sheriff's men, one of they baillies or magistrates, I should think.'

'Don't take me amiss, Mister Kemp, but have you ever been in the tollbooth?'

'It was a long time since.'

'Aye, for sure. Who put ye there?'

'It was just the one night. I was fou' an' fechtin'. I canna rightly call to mind but I was before the magistrate and made to pay a fine.'

There was laughter and some mocking at the picture that was being built up of this frail and grass-coloured old creature being arrested for being drunk and disorderly. James called them to order.

'Aye, just so. I merely wished to be sure that you know that no ordinary man can put anybody to the tollbooth. If these men threatened you, and you believed that they could do what they said, then they might have been Sheriff's men, or the baillies themselves. I'm not saying that they were, mind, I'm just wondering why you believed them.'

'Aye, well as you say. I did believe them and I let them take my son back, although against my will. And, do you know, that when I made complaint to those that were concerned in yon ship *The Planter*, saying that it was a shame and a scandal that young boys should be taken to serve overseas, do you know what happened? The very same people, they shipowners, merchants and baillies and so forth, they sent the drum through the town of Aberdeen proclaiming a prohibition to those they employed, not to engage or indent any such boys – but, nonetheless, I could not get my boys back. Now what do you think of that, mister law-clerk, for a piece of hypocrisy?'

Above the hubbub of agreement, shouting and stamping from the assembly in the room, James had just two more things to ask. He needed to be sure that this was the noose before asking the kidnappers to put it around their necks. He found himself breathing hard and his hand shaking.

'You had both boys taken? How old were they?'

125

'The younger one, James, was but eleven year old, when he was taken. How it came about I cannot tell, for I was confined to my bed with pains in my legs, that I could not move. My wife went to the merchants, but after the pother over Peter they paid her no heed. The bairn was put on board another ship that sailed the same day as Captain Ragg, but I know not what name it had nor the name of any captain, nor man who listed him, nor did I have any means by which to get him back again.

'How old was Peter?'

'When he was taken? Thirteen. He's thirty-two years old now and married with a fine son of his own. We never talk of those days.'

'You've seen him then? He came back?' The noise had abated a little now and glasses were being re-filled and chairs scraped over the floor. James could well hear what the painter was saying.

'Och, aye. He cam' back. Yon Indian Peter with his drummin' an' dancin' an' bookwriting is no' the only man to come hame. My Peter was put in service to a shipmaster and merchant beyond seas, do you see? And now he works the ships himsel' forbye he's a sailor, and soon to be a ship's mate, so he tells me.'

'Mister Kemp, I said you were a wonder! You have made my day a good one after all. It would make me even happier if you were to tell me that your son, Peter, were even now in Aberdeen and agreeable to come and speak with me as you have done.'

'You may be a happy man, sir, for indeed the sailor is home from the sea.'

'Then will you ask him for me? Say that I will be staying here a two-three days, and would be glad to take a dram with him.'

'I will do better than that for he will be with me the morn. Will I ask him tae pay his respects tae ye?'

'Aye, for sure. I'll not keep him long. God be with you, John Kemp.'

The two men shook hands, one green with paint, one freckled with age. James handed the painter his bit of blanket and watched him shuffling away through the crowd of drinkers and out into the cold.

*

126

'Unless it was a lean year and times hard.'

'Or the breadwinner died that would have cared for his family.'

'There was one boy I ken, was only seven when his father died and his uncle sent him to Virginia to some friends.'

'Do you remember Charles Ewan was given a sucket, a piece of biscuit and a dram, and then they promised him a new coat and other great encouragement if he would sign on to go?'

'Aye and he ran away to think it over.'

'And was told he was a fool and that he would be sold to black men who would eat him!'

'Did he believe that?'

'Well, he didna' go, that's for sure!'

There was no sign of the crowd breaking up, nor the topic of conversation being exhausted. James was tired, the climax of his nervousness had passed, and the satisfaction of work well done in his masters' service was a warm and drowsy heaviness that sapped his energy. He stretched and stood up to shake the stiffness from his fingers and straighten his back. Perhaps too this was the moment to leave the room, for his bladder was beginning to insist that he was an old man after all. But someone else had taken the floor, and before James could catch the moment and make a run for it she had sent her challenge echoing round the room

'Na, na. It's no' for the hard times, but they will sail when they've a mind tae it and if it's a two-three bairns needful to make up their cargo, then they'll take the first that comes by and no speirin' who's to sign for them.'

'Margaret Ingram from Loanhead,' George whispered. 'If'n anybody has a tale to tell it's this woman.'

'You've heard me many a time sinsyne, lamenten an' greetin for the loss o' my son. I'm an old woman now, and James was our only bairn, the child of our middle years, John and me. He was no' a scholar and there was those that called him Daft Jamie, but he was a good boy and would have stayed with his mother and been a comfort to her, the more just now, when I'm a widow-woman and no man to look to. I did but send him on a message the half mile into Aberdeen and he was taken up by that Alexander Gray that calls himself a merchant. A merchant of slavery is what I say, for Jamie

127

was only twelve year old, and younger in his wits; and they took him and they hid him and it was eight day before my man could come at him. But come Sunday, we were at the kirk to hear worship and who did I see but my son, dunten a muckle drum, shauchling the streets, his shoes half aff, an' a load o' villains, wi' childer an' wild queans behind. But we fetched him aff and back home and kept him within door for some time, until four buirdly fella's cam' tae oor bed in the nicht, when we were sleepin' an' Jamie at the feet o' us, and they took hold of him, and when we speired for why, they tellt us they were from Alexander Gray and they'd to take Jamie awa'. An' when the bairn heert it, he skailed and wept tears, but, will he nill he, he must go with them and they drew him from his bed and carried him awa'. But his fayther followed and saw where they cam', to Gray's house, and we'd to get a letter from a magistrate, or e'er we could come at him again.'

Long ago it may have been, and an often repeated episode, but the old woman kilted up her skirts and, quite without embarrassment in that company, blew her nose and wiped her eyes on her ample petticoats. Nobody stirred. There was little to be gained from reminding her about the rules of evidence. This was her story, polished in the telling, and narrated for this audience in this place. They held the silence unbroken until she had straightened her gown and could go on.

'An' that was no' the end o'it, for they'd stripped him naked so he'd not run aff, and I'd to wrap him in my plaid for to take him hame. And after I'd kept him by me a whole while, he was into the town again, and taken again. Only this time it was by a foxy fellow that went by the name of Lunen, Dod Lunen. Well, he took him up and he was put into the tollbooth wi' criminals and evil men, and I could not fetch him awa'. His fayther went a-looking but the men whipped Jamie away. I went and I went, I begged and I prayed, but all I could do for the bairn was to gie him ma blessin' afore he was taken to the Plantations, and I never seen him again.'

And this time Margaret Ingram's tears ran openly down her cheeks and she made no attempt to wipe them away.

'They say it was a time of hardship, provisions very dear and scarce and many were difficulted to get their bread... They say that he was over the age of schooling... They say that he had signed for to go and he was breaking his agreement, but he was our only son, and hard times are no new thing. We would have kept him fed and clothed, whatever betide, and as for schooling, he never did go to school, nor could he sign his name, so how could their "agreement", if ever there was one, be any agreement in law? So, mister, if you have come here with the intention to get the law on our behalf, then listen well: these men, Gray and Garioch and Lunen and Smith and all others like them, they would whistle up the devil to swear they had the law on their side, but there's no law on God's earth that lets them take wee boys away from their parents and send them to be slaves on the other side of the world.'

If there was no applause for this fine speech, there was agreement and murmuring and deep sighs. Every eye was turned towards James and it seemed that some reply was expected from him. He looked round from one face to another. These people depended on him. This action, this whole process, was not just for Peter, but for all those others like Margaret Ingram who had tried to get magistrates' letters, who had laid out money they could ill afford, to buy back indentures and who, in the end could only give their blessing to their lost children. And it was for those others – whole families from the high hills beyond – driven in harshness from their homes, the land turned over to bracken and sour weeds, while they sold themselves into hard labour in a strange land. He had known this all along; he had known it with his mind and because Peter had felt it so strongly; but now, surrounded by these people, he realized that he knew it in his soul. He did not answer, because there was nothing he could say that did not sound like a platitude or the empty promise of some politician.

At that moment, at the centre of the silence, the door opened and two newcomers entered the room, a man and a woman. Behind them, in the doorway, was the man who, earlier, had slipped away so silently.

Chapter 19

Everyone turned round to look and a whisper of recognition ran through the group. The spy returned outside and closed the street door. James, seizing the opportunity, made a quick dash out of the small door behind him, that led to the rest of the house, leaving George to sort out who these people were and whether it was anything to do with his affairs. His undignified exit may have given the wrong impression to the folk who so needed him for their champion, but there was nothing he could do about it. He barely made it to the yard as it was. Having relieved himself, he entered the room again to find the whole scene changed. Like a stage set, the previous focus of attention had been on his chair and his table. Those people who had spoken had, by instinct, left the audience and come to a point beside him, where they could hold the attention of the entire room. Without deliberate arrangement on his part, the evening had been played as if set in a court of law. Now the people had turned around, and the focus of attention was all on these two strangers. James entered to a call and a finger pointed at him as if he was the accused.

'James Maclaurin, are you associated with this jailbird, Peter Williamson?'

'The whole city of Aberdeen is associated with Peter Williamson.'

'This is no place for lawyers' quibbling. The man may be an Indian king or any other great man for all I know, but he is banished the city for his lies. He daresn't show his own face, so what does he do? He sends you to go poking around for more rumours and vicious tittle-tattle. Now, we two have come to set the picture straight, to bear witness of the truth! So, get your papers out and write this down, law clerk!'

The man who spoke was not immediately prepossessing nor authoritative. He was soft and butter-coloured with expressive hands

130

that were tanned pale orange. His coat was also splodged a buttery orange and his hair was orange-brown and wispy, for he wore neither wig nor hat. The woman with him detached herself from his side and went to get a glass of ale; she was a rounded body, dark haired and dark skinned, almost like a gipsy, even to the bright neckerchief that she wore instead of a shawl. She swung her way back with two large glasses and sat beside her companion. James wondered if they were man and wife, but had no time for further speculation, since not only the stranger but all those in the room seemed to be waiting for what was to come. The man stabbed a long finger at the papers on the table and waited for James to begin. For a moment the old clerk wondered whether he should defy the rude onslaught, but decided that, in his present tiredness and with only the unpredictable backing of the crowd, he would do better to give in than to protest.

'Write this: James Smith, saddler in Aberdeen, aged about fifty-five years, depones that...' Maclaurin looked up quickly. How did this man know how to make such a deposition? Had he done this before? ... 'Write man! Put it down just as I say; you can question me after. Depones that: in the year one thousand seven hundred and forty-three, the deponent was spoke to about the affair of indenting servants to go to America on board Captain Ragg's ship, *The Planter*. The deponent is very positive that nobody did ever desire or insinuate to the deponent to engage or indent any girls or boys under age for that purpose, nor did any of the gentlemen concerned in that enterprise ever desire, suggest or mention to the deponent to kidnap, deceive or circumveen any boys or girls or any other person or persons whatsoever, to engage, inlist or indent to go to America, on board the said ship *The Planter*, for the account of the owners or the Master of the said ship; nor does the deponent understand that ever any such purpose or practice was intended by them. Am I going too fast for you?'

James scrabbled for the last few words. His legal shorthand, thank the Lord, was not too rusty for the occasion.

'...that ever any such purpose or practice ... No, Mister Smith, I have it all. I am peculiarly grateful to you for giving your deposition so expertly. I take it that this is not the first time you have given evidence in this way.'

He did not dare to look up from his papers, nor to catch the eye of any of the audience in the room, but he heard the rustle of amusement that followed his question and prayed that there would be no open laughter from them. He wanted to keep them on his side without unduly provoking this saddler who stood across from him, with the bark-stained hands of his trade spread in a mocking question. He did not speak, however, and James plunged on.

'I have only the one question... No, I have two questions. Did you personally supervise those people whom you employed to enlist servants?'

'No, of course I didna'. If they are to give evidence it's their affair.'

No justification, thought Maclaurin, no explanation. This man, if his deposition is to be challenged, will have to be ensnared first. A soft man, with a shell-like armour around him; best left to others to deal with, if he could be brought to court.

'I have asked this of some of the others, so I must ask it of you – and you too, mistress. Would you be prepared to attend the Court of Session in Edinburgh to answer questions upon this your evidence? You can be summoned, in which case you *must* attend, or I can ask you questions here, before all these people and put your answers into your deposition to go before the Lord Ordinary.'

A very small thorn to pierce his armour, thought Maclaurin and waited for Smith to reply.

'Tell it now! Let's see what you have to say before this company. Was it you threatened James Kemp wi' a club? What about those that was in the tollbooth? How much did they pay you? Can you swear that none of these children were under age? Did you ask them? Who signed the papers? Did you have their parents' consent?'

The fury of the small crowd in the room seemed to boil around them. James was as much concerned about the safety of Smith at that moment, as he was about getting the depositions down. In the event it was the gipsy-woman who came in to the centre of the storm and stilled it with one toss of her head.

'Haud yer whisht, the lot o' ye! There's nae guid to come frae hammering the puir man like that. Ye ken fine wha's behind all this an' it's no' James Smith, I'm no' aimin' to defend him; I'm no' aimin' to defend anybody. It's nothing but the truth will serve this day, an' the truth is that folk like him an me, we earnt our money keeping

132

indented servants warm an' fed for all the long days till the ships were ready to sail. We were paid to do it, and we, in our turn, paid others. If any of yous think that we should have known – by magic, no doubt – who was twelve year old and who was fourteen, or divined, by reading the wind, who had been taken by force and who was dragged back by force after runnin' away on purpose to get taken on somewheres else, then answer me this. Who kept the papers? Who attested the indentures? Who gave us our orders? Who do you think should have made sure everything was legal and above board? When ye've answered that then ye'll have the truth o' it.'

She turned to James and said, quite calmly, 'They'll not answer, and you'll get no more from us. You're the wise man to hold your court performance in Edinburgh, for there's none here would try the law on those that make the law. Do you want to hear my deposition?'

Smith, the saddler, turned upon his heel and left the room. Nobody stopped him; hardly anyone turned to see him go. All eyes were on his former companion. Now that she had come nearer to him, James could see that the woman he had taken for a gipsy was in fact much older than she had seemed at first. Her hair was black still, maybe by use of walnut juice for it was a dense, dark, unrelieved colour all through. Her strong body was set in solid weight, and she commanded rather than seduced attention. James took up his pen in readiness.

'My name is Helen Law, spouse to William Soper, wool comber. My age is sixty years or thereby. Between the years seventeen forty and seventeen forty-six, at least several servants – boys and girls, men and women – were indented and engaged by merchants in this city to go and serve in America. I can give you the names of those merchants.' She counted them off on her fingers. 'George and Andrew Garioch, Alexander Gray, James Abernethy, George Black...' She clicked her finger several times... 'someone Copland, Captain Ragg and even James Smith, who's just left the room, all stationed and boarded servants with me.

'I have a good memory, Mister. Listen to this; this should satisfy ye. I can recall that among those boarded with me was a boy that was sometimes called Peter Williamson and sometimes Peter McWilliam! Isna' he the fellow causing all this trouble? Well, let me put you straight. All the boys that Smith's men brought in were put into a

133

house in the same close with the workhouse, to which house I brought their victuals to them. Some of those servants boarded by Smith who had been in the tollbooth for some crime before he engaged them were still kept in the tollbooth; the boys were in the close with the workhouse; the women in my own house, until they were all sent over to Tory. I took a house in Tory to cook their victuals in, but there was a great many more people boarded with me and got their victuals with me in Tory than I had in Aberdeen. And then one day, which was some months later and just before she sailed, I left some blankets on board the ship, and I'd to go on board *The Planter* myself to fetch away the blankets, and I took some gingerbread and tobacco which I distributed amongst my boarders, and they begged me to go along with them to America and cook their victuals on the passage, which I told them it was not in my power to do, but not one of those boarders of mine made any complaint, but still insisted that I should go along with them. And there was some of them, the little ones, that said they were going to a country to eat sugar and to drink wine...'

'What do you mean, "little ones"?'

James had been too busy writing to pick up on that point. It was one of the women in the room who had interrupted the unpunctuated flow of Helen Law's story. One by one, other women, and men too, began to call questions.

'What little ones? Boys do you mean? How little were they, for God's sake? Did you know how old they were? Did any of them ever say they'd been taken by force? James Smith, your friend, who's gone and left ye to face the music here, did he or any of his men use threats or force on these little ones?'

Helen Law looked genuinely surprised at being challenged. There was an air of comfortable self-righteousness about her that defied indignation.

'I was like a mother to those boys!'

'But they'd mothers of their own. Did you never think they might have been snatched from their real mothers?'

'I know nothing about that. I never heard any of my boarders, old or young, on any occasion or at any time, complain that they had been kidnapped or taken up by force. On the contrary, they said they were very lucky to be going to a better country, and they wanted me to go with them.'

'Then why did you no'?'

'I was a married woman, with a man to care for, and boys of my own.'

'They were no' kidnapped, I'll warrant!'

'There was my eldest son was enlisted by James Abernethie to go, but when I applied to Abernethie to have him dispensed with the boy insisted that he would go. So he re-enlisted with the same man, and went to America.'

'And what age was your son? Did he cry for his mammy? Was he taken in the streets and locked up in a barn?'

'He was fifteen years old, bigger than many, and of a mind of his own. I never saw any locked up, in a barn or elsewhere, unless they'd run away.'

'Run away? So they did try to get away? What for would they do that, do you think? If they were happy to go, to eat sugar and drink wine and have a better life, why would they run off?'

James felt that it was high time that he intervened. Although in many respects she was a hostile witness, she was so full of incident and had such good recall that any advocate worth his salt would get her admitting to murder before too long.

'Mistress Law, I would not have you put on trial here. This is no court, for all your name is Law!'

He was ashamed of the pun, but at this stage he would say anything just to lighten the mood. The audience tittered; he was on home ground.

'What is on trial, is the truth of Peter Williamson's story, and that will be heard in another place.'

He had diverted the stream, no doubt, but the flood gates were open and wrath poured out upon his head.

'What about us? Is there no law against taking ... trepanning ... kidnapping ... whatever ye'd call it, that will give us our rights? Did ye' no' hear, Mister? Yon' Williamson, wi' his fine feathers and his singin' and dancin' in the streets, is no' but a chained bear, sufferin' for our entertainment. If he's to be heard in the courts and then the likes of her come along sayin' it was all sugar and wine, where's the court that will hear what we have to say? Will your lords ordinary in their fine gowns hear we poor folk in our grievance?'

'I don't know. The law has to be invoked. It does not move of itself.'

'Then you move it!'

'I cannot do that. I'm a servant of the law – an old servant of the law. I'm no lawyer, I'm only a clerk. I'm writing down what you say, but I'm not what you'd call a Writer. There's those that are ... Writers to the Signet ... they can move the law. It's not for me to do.'

'Then let yon Williamson move it. If he can do for himself, let him have some care for others!'

'I hear you and ye've given me cause for thought. When I go back to my masters in Edinburgh, I'll see what may be done.'

May God forgive me, he thought, I sound like a canting minister, promising joy to the poor and suffering. Don't they know that the world's justice is not constructed for righting wrong, but only for establishing the rule of law? How can James Maclaurin and Peter Williamson change the world?

In spite of the high rush of excitement in George Mackie's place that night, and in spite of his lowness in the face of it all, James woke the next morning with a sense of purpose. In spite of what had been said, in spite of all the emotion of the night before, he would content himself with his trade. He would go about his masters' affairs without taking on the business of the world. Let Peter worry about the ethics of it all; his responsibility was to gather evidence, not to decide how the law would use it.

Chapter 20

Robert Thomson, Town Clerk, in his austere but warmly fire-lit room was grimly welcoming to the visiting law-clerk. He knew exactly how to deal with such persons and would be glad to be of assistance. He dipped quill pen in the inkpot and looked enquiringly at James.

'How may I help?'

'I think you may have been guilty of theft.'

Not a muscle twitched; the man's composure was extraordinary.

'Really – and what makes you think that?'

'I think you have in your room here, three hundred and fifty copies of a pamphlet with some pages cut out and burnt by the common hangman, and three hundred and fifty copies of another pamphlet, complete, no pages cut out or burnt, both the property of Peter Williamson, planter, late of Philadelphia.'

'And do you see these pamphlets, hereabouts?'

'No.'

'But you still think that they are here?'

'I think they had better be here, or somewhere safe, so that they can be returned in good order to their owner.'

'I see. Would you excuse me one moment?'

Smooth and cool as ever, Thomson went to the door that led to the outer office and murmured something. Returning to his desk he did not sit down but stood, looming by the fireplace.

'I have asked for the whereabouts of the works you mention to be ascertained, but as I am sure you will understand, Mister ... Maclaurin, I can in no way let you have these papers. If they are in my possession, it is by order of the Court and I would therefore need the Court's permission to release them to you.'

'I quite understand. While we are waiting, Mr Thomson, I wonder if you could just tell me whether it was indeed yourself that wrote out a missive, directed to the magistrates and intended to be published, that was signed, after some persuasion, by Williamson himself.'

'It is possible that I may have done so, at the behest of the Procurator-Fiscal.'

'That is the Dean of Guild, Alexander Cushnie?'

'Acting as Procurator-Fiscal, as is his right.'

'Yes, indeed. Did you also witness the burning of the books, Mr Thomson?'

'It would have been my duty to do so.'

At that moment he was called outside and, although he did not close the door, James could not hear what was said. There was a considerable pause and then a strange, wizened old scrivener, quill pen behind one ear, the very caricature of a humble clerk appeared, wheezing that Mr Thomson had been unavoidably called away but that anyway there was nothing more that he could do for Mr Maclaurin – so 'good day'.

James left, satisfied that the books were indeed there, and satisfied also that Thomson, whilst he had not lied, had carefully avoided telling the truth. He was also certain that the news of his presence and the reason for his mission would soon be common knowledge. Here was yet another cause of haste. Suddenly he realized that he was on a different stair to the one he had come in by. The old building was a warren of passages and stairways. There was a door on the landing below that stood ajar admitting light, seemingly to provide safe passage on the dark stairs, just as it picked out in gold letters that this was the office of the Town-Clerk-Depute, Walter Cochran. He availed himself of the glimmer to go on towards the side entrance that he could see below him.

Cochran! Oh, no! He stopped, one foot in mid-air, ridiculous as a comic drawing. It was not possible that fate had played him a winning hand of this magnitude. He crept back, and there it was, painted on the door. He knocked and walked in.

The only figure in the room was a small shape against the window. Cochran could not have been much above five feet tall, his head barely above sill-height. On James' entrance he whirled round and then smiled. His face was charming, regular featured, smooth-skinned – a child, of fifty or so years. What he must have been like when he

138

was young, and what straits he must have put himself to to get taken as a full grown man, with that angelic appearance James could not guess. But here he was, smiling his welcome, with genuine pleasure.

'Did you want to see me? Most people go on by, but my door is always open as you can see. Now, what may I do for you?'

James sat himself down and introduced himself as collecting information concerning the insurance of *The Planter*.

'It seems that there may be some sums owing to the sharers on account of the wreck. Your name appears, with others, on the brieve. It is not, you understand, the vessel herself, but the cargo. I have been to see Patrick Barron...'

'Ah yes, but he came late into the venture and I think was able to get some recompense for the loss of his furniture, and, of course, he will have had his share of the sale of servants, even though he had no part in that side of the enterprise.'

'I think he is well satisfied. He seemed to be more concerned with present than past shipments.'

'A very industrious and worthwhile citizen is Patrick Barron.'

'You yourself now. Would you have had dealings with the indented servants? It is possible, do you see, that any person who might claim legitimate expense with regard to these servants might have a greater claim on the insurance money.'

'But the claim has been settled. It is some years now.'

'Such matters can never be entirely settled and finished. You must know that the law is somewhat of a slow train and a long fuse which may blow up at any time and surprise us all. That is why I am here, Mr Cochran. I can promise nothing, but it may be worth trying. What can you lose? If you had aught to do with the indenting of servants then you may be due some recompense. Can you cast your mind back?'

'I can do better than that. I am only Town-Clerk-Depute but I know the value of written records and good book keeping.'

Cochran, who had remained standing, went to a cupboard in the panelling and, unlocking it with a small key that hung with others on a silver chain from his short, fashionable waistcoat, produced a small red book. He showed James the fly leaf on which was written in a clear script: 'Account between Baillie William Fordyce and company and James Smith, Saddler of Aberdeen, for the Recruiting of Servants. Jan 1743 – May 1743'.

'This will tell us all we need to know. Now you must understand I am no merchant, but Robert Ragg is my cousin and, as a man of some property, I came in to the business one of the first; besides, my civic duties are not so pressing but that I could not find time to assist my relative. A return cargo of tobacco would have made us all rich men, but, as it is, I suppose I lost somewhat more than many of the others by paying for the keep of the servants all that winter until the weather was fit for the journey. Aye, you see here, there is eighteen pounds paid to Smith to go to Inverness to enlist servants, and here a sum for candle, peats, straw, et cetera, for those in the tollbooth, and to Helen Law for the diet of servants. Certain it is that we'd laid out a tolerable sum for the keep of these enlisted men before ever we saw any profit. As the vessel was then grounded, we lost not only the possibility of profitable tobacco but all the pre-payment for the keep of these convicts and servants, as well as the victualling of the ship for their safe transport. If aught is owed, then to be sure I am owed as well.'

'These servants now... Do you have a list, showing how many there were, or even their names?'

'I may have made a note of the numbers, somewhere ... names even, where necessary.'

At that moment the door was thrust open.

'Cochran, there's been a man here after the books taken from... What are you doing here? Why are you still on the premises? This is not the proper way out. What have you said to him, Walter?'

The veneer of icy politeness had disappeared entirely. Thomson was in a fury and showed his teeth in a snarl at James.

'This man is an informer. A paid spy in the employ of Peter Williamson that we banished the city! The villain's too afraid to come himself, so he sends this old, quavering poltroon to stir up trouble. I hope you said nothing to him.'

'What could he say?' James was feeling far from bold, but that 'old, quavering poltroon' description had affronted his dignity. 'Is there something you are afraid of?'

Thomson was regaining his composure. 'Na, na. Of course, you are quite right. There is nothing for us to get concerned about. The law will take care of everything. It is, after all, one of the rules of jurisprudence that you have to believe your client is innocent, just as we are certain that the man is guilty. Anything my depute may have said is, naturally, only his opinion, is not that so, Walter?'

Cochran seemed disinclined to answer.

'We talked of ships and insurance. The subject of Peter Williamson never came into it.' James looked to see whether Cochran had made any connection between the two, but he was still smiling the same sweet smile. Quavering poltroon or no, James thought it time to go. 'I have other business to attend to. I bid you good day, gentlemen.'

He was somewhat surprised that they let him walk out unmolested. But there was no sound from either of the men and no sound as he went down the stairs. Coming from the dark entrance into a side alley, he blinked in the winter cold, and for a moment could not get his bearings. However, he stepped out into the main street briskly, any way he could to seem busy and undisturbed by what had happened.

The thoughts inside his head were very disturbing. He needed to sort them out. 'Andrew Crosbie could never have imagined anything like this when he sent me north,' he muttered. The extreme of Thomson's anger was overwhelming and smelt like fear, especially when added to the speed of the magistrates' actions against Peter, for they had jailed, banished and humiliated him all within twenty-four hours. They had talked of conspiracy and perverting the course of justice in Edinburgh, and then it had seemed like normal court procedure, but now, in these cold, raw streets with the stuff of commerce all about him, his mind ran on piracy, violence and the robbers and reivers of fiction. He began to talk to himself, in a way that had become common in him since Margaret died.

'You're afeared, James Maclaurin; afeared an' pissing wi' cowardice. Brace yoursel' an' ponder on this: they'll not harm ye' – they daresn't. But ye'd best lie low for a while. Ye've stirred up a hornet's nest and no mistake.'

Like a homing bird he found his way back to Mackie's and collapsed into a chair. It was too early for there to be many people in the public rooms, and George, seeing his pallor and exhaustion, exclaimed over him and rubbed spirits into his bald head and warmed his feet by the fire and plied him with barley gruel, plentifully laced with brandy.

'Peter should never have gone off and left ye. Och I ken fine you sent him awa' an I unnerstand whyfore, but, man, you look like you'd been visited! You're too old for such tricks. Now I've a natural, human visitor for ye' in the next room, but I'll send him away if ye've a mind to yer bed. What do you say?'

'I'll see him – of course I will. Would you let him come in here? And, George, thank you for your care of me. I'll stay in doors a while if I may, for I believe that there are those who may want to cause trouble, but I do not want to bring harm to you. You've been warned off once, when Peter was banished, but now we need you safe and we need your testimony; so you can say I've left the city if you like.'

'I'll do no such thing. Warned off, you say? Nobody warns me off. I've no need to lick spittle nor kiss the boots of any man. If'n I send the brand out, there's Mackies enow in this city to fetch the hide off any thieving Sheriff, magistrate or Town-bawdy-Clerk, beggin' your pardon, James.'

'My hand on it, you're a fine gentleman an' I feel at hame here. Tell me one thing though before I see yon visitor. Who is Baillie Fordyce?'

'Captain William Fordyce of Aquhorties, JP. A merchant, and a powerful influence hereby. He was made a captain in the forty-five.'

'Tell me more.'

'The town was put in "a posture of defence" ... and some o' they grand citizens still give themselves title although it was six year ago, an naethin to boast of. There's a host of captens and ensigns. Let's see if I can recall ... They meet here sometimes to put on their fine clothes and jaw and drink the loyal toast. There's Provost John Robertson, that calls himself Major, an' there's a whole mess of captens: John Elphinston, John Burnet and Alexander Mitchell, as well as Fordyce; the Lieutenants – Charles Forbes of Shiels, the Sheriff substitute, Charles Copland and James Black – and the ensigns are Peter Barron and William Crystall. All well kennt and respected, and woe betide if you don't give proper title and rank ... God save King George, and drink confusion to his enemies!'

142

'I'm grateful, George, very grateful. You're a good man. The warmth has come back to me and I'm ready for anything. Who's your visitor now?

Chapter 21

Peter Williamson rode back in triumph, carrying a copy of his baptism record, a certificate from the united parishes of Aboyne and Glentanner and sworn statements from Francis Fraser, Peter Cromar and John Wilson. Many another, he knew, would testify for him if asked, but he did not think it would ever be necessary to call them all the way to the Scottish capital when he had such firm testimony to give Andrew. What chance had the magistrates now to say he had lied? What chance had they of justifying his imprisonment and humiliation? Even the old horse seemed to sense his good humour for he pricked up his ears and managed a brisk canter from time to time, on his way back to his own warm stable. There were starlings whistling in the fields and a hare with whitened coat lolloped away from the roadside. Peter felt like a hero!

He did not bother to stop to change the stirrups back. Let them think what they would at the livery stable. He hoped that he and James would not be long in Aberdeen. It was not because of the danger of discovery; he was too confident to be afraid. It was only that, having achieved the major part of his task, he was in a hurry to get on with the lawsuit.

He found James sitting warm and snug by the fire, drinking with a tall fair-haired sailor. They were laughing together, with a jug of ale in the hearth and papers strewn all around. Peter felt a strong wave of resentment, indeed he was plain angry. He wanted to boast of his triumph and sweep James off to Edinburgh and the Court of Sessions without a moment's delay, and here he found the old man carousing with sailors and expecting him to be sociable and pass the time of day with strangers.

'Look who's here, Peter. Look well and tell me who you see.'

'Who? Don't you mean what? I can see you swallowing down sea

144

tales and quaffing ale with our papers strewn helter-skelter about the room.'

He dragged the old man up by the arm and took him aside. 'Why are you wasting time? Are you not ready to hear what I have done? Look at this. This is proof. We have it all now! I can prove I was taken by force, I can prove that I was only twelve at the time and I have sworn statements to say that my father looked for me! But what ails you?'

'Oh, I'm well enough. Just bide a wee while and see what we have here... Peter Williamson, this is Peter Kemp.'

'Man you're fou... Peter who? Peter Kemp! Stookie! But I saw ye sold for a slave in Philadelphia! What the devil do you make here? Oh man, I canna believe it! Stookie!'

Peter threw his arms around the sailor in a huge embrace and it would be hard to say which of the two men looked the more surprised. The tall sailor quickly broke loose, embarrassed at this sudden affection from someone who was so obviously a stranger.

'Don't you know me, Stookie? I was on *The Planter* alsweel. Oh I'd ken yon straw thatch of yours anywhere. I'm Peter Williamson that was kidnapped here and held in the barn. You must remember – there was Kirsty and Jamie, and you and me, took all our meals together and...

'Peter Williamson you say.' He turned to Maclaurin. 'Oh, I'd heard that it was by cause of this play-actor that you were speirin' for tales of servants and taking by force and the rest of that draff? Well I was on *The Planter* and I well remember a wee bit fellow called himself Williamson, was for aye maundering on about how he'd been kidnapped and how he would be sure to get home and have his revenge. Well ... Now you see there's two of us made our way back. No great heroes, and no so bad for all that's gone by, so there's an end!'

'Stookie, you canna just leave me after so long a time? Don't you recognize me? Is there nothing you can see about me that says to you I'm the same fellow you went with to the New World?'

'Mebbe ay, mebbe no. Who's to say?'

'But you remember ... you must remember something! What about the wreck? You must recall how we went ashore when the crew deserted, and how they came back with a boat to take us to be sold?'

145

'I remember – of course I remember! I've said I was there. But you and my father are trying to make me say things your way. My father is an old man and given to fancies, whereas you...'

James signed to Peter to hold his peace and not to reply. There was much to be gained from the sailor and no time for quarrels.

'Your father has told me what he remembers but, of a certainty you would be better placed to set events in their due order. Would you sit down again and let us hear what you have to tell. You have said that you were on *The Planter* when she set sail from Aberdeen in the year 1743?'

'Aye, or thereabouts.'

'Well, we'll need to be a little more precise. I have assurances that she set sail in May 1743 and made but the one voyage, so if you were on board then it was certainly in that year. Who got ye to go?'

'I enlisted.'

'Aye. Fine. What was the name of the man who enlisted ye?'

'It was James Smith. He was employed by the owners of the ship to take servants.'

'You say "take servants". Does that mean that you...?'

'No, you misunderstand! I know what my father says but I placed myself in his care. There was no force used. See here, Mister...'

'Maclaurin.'

'Mister Maclaurin, my father and I were always at each other for the one thing... How soon would I come into the business with him? He was for ever maundering on about how he had built it up for his boys, and how... You'd think, Mister, that we were God's gift to him, put on this earth for no other purpose than to paint! And no' to paint pretty pictures! Not even to choose the colours! No, we were there to follow in his footsteps. Man, you've seen him; he's still at it, a reproof incarnate, old and sick and still covering surfaces, protecting from the salt wind and the sun. Taunting me, for that I will not join him. But I was never the man for those ways, nor my brother neither. If there's a salt wind blowing, I'm for feeling it in my face; and if the sun is to shine, then I'm all for having it shine on me in some other place than cold, grey Aberdeen. If my father says that I was kept from him and he'd the devil's own job to get me back, then he says true. I would sooner serve Auld Hornie himself than serve paint and brushes to my father in a life of slavery!'

'But were you not a slave in America?'

'But under new skies and learning new ways. There's no too much green paint in the New World. Out there, all you see of green is the trees and the tall, green corn. Out there, the houses are all painted white.'

This man is a poet, thought Maclaurin. No wonder you could not cage him, James Kemp. You were a fool to try.

Peter Williamson was lost, on the edges of what to him seemed like a shadow show, or some scene acted behind a lighted window. He could hear everything, but distantly, as an outsider. The anger and resentment that he had felt when he first came in, had not diminished. He warmed his spirits at it and kept it burning, but now it was directed at the space that was growing between himself and the old law clerk, between himself and this sailor who had shared his adversity but gloried in it. He wanted to shout; he wanted to impose his story on these events. Everything seemed to be getting further away from his control, as if he had no role to play, as if some other author had taken over his script.

Peter Kemp was going on with his part...

'I had thought to serve five years, but my indentures were lost in the wreck and so I served for seven. But I've no regrets. To be sure there's little honour in being a slave. Over there they thought us all convicts and we were treated as such, but I was well enough for all that. I passed through several hands until I found myself given a berth with a ship-wright, and from there I took to the sea. Times the life of a sailor has little comfort in it – but I've no ties, only a wife and bairns to come home to. I've seen a fair proportion of the world and a great deal of salt water.'

'And the salt wind to blow in your face?'

'And the salt wind to blow in my face.'

Williamson looked at the other Peter and saw a stranger. He had tried to see in this tall man with the fierce eyes and thin, unsmiling mouth, the laughing boy who had taken life so blithely in the barn. Now he was smiling again, but not with him; it was at James that he smiled, at their shared secret. The fierce jealousy that fuelled his anger could not be contained longer.

'I'll see if George can find me something to eat. I've been in the saddle all day. Good day to you, Peter Kemp. I remember you, even if you've forgotten all about me.'

James looked at him enquiringly, but said nothing. There was an undue ferocity in the younger man's voice and in the way he swept from the room. No doubt he was tired after his journey. The old man saw the sailor out and began to gather up the papers that littered the room. Although he never cared much for order or luxury in his own surroundings, he liked orderly thinking, and these papers represented for him the disorder of human feelings: the stress between father and son, the grief over neglectful children, of bereavement and unfinished scenes of turmoil. He could, and would, establish some kind of order. He could, and would, put these testaments into the third person and, by so doing, remove the pain from them... But not now... Now there were bigger fish to fry and he was fearful. He was beginning to get some idea of the forces that lay behind the evidence he had gathered the night before. Today's encounters had opened his eyes to something more menacing.

When Peter returned, washed and fed, but with a hot, tight face, that showed the anger below the surface, James plunged straight in...

'Peter, there's much we have to tell each other, but there's ill ahead and I'm afeared. While you were away I've stirred up trouble over your arrest and there's no doubt but that they will be after ridding themselves of the two of us as soon as maybe. We might have to disappear from sight, and yet... Peter, sit by awhile... You've the first bit of your story straight and proven and there's much there that Andrew will make hay with in court, but I've a feeling that there's more to this than a simple case of wrongful arrest.'

'Why? Is that not enough for you? I was right and they were wrong. They'll have no chance against haymaker Andrew with all the evidence I have against them.'

'Haven't I just said as much? But be still and whisht! I've no time now to tell you all that I've heard and seen, but I've been sitting here with the hairs prickling on the back of my neck, and not from the cold neither. I went to the office of the Town Clerk and when I came out I was afeared, and all day since, the fear has been growing, and d'you know why? Because all I did was ask for the return of your

148

book, and yet they were afraid! They were afraid of you, and afraid of what you said in your book, and what you might say if you came back.'

'But surely that's what we want, is it not? What if they are afraid? What harm can they do, with the law on our side?'

'Think again, Peter, and think clear. First ask yourself: Why are the authorities so afraid? They had to discredit you and everything you said, and they took extreme measures to stop you and to stop anyone taking you seriously, and they made the punishment very public. Now, when I ask myself the same question, the only answer I can give is that they are afraid because they themselves are guilty. Guilty because *they* are the men behind the shipping of servants, guilty because in the end it is *they* who are responsible for your kidnap and, above all, guilty of the kidnap of many more young people besides yourself.'

'What? The Town Clerk and the Sheriff and the Dean of Guild? Guilty against the law? But they *are* the law!'

'Now do you see why the hairs stand on my nape and my knees fail?'

'But this is better and better! Why are you fashing yourself with turncoat safety-seekers like Peter Kemp when, if you're right, Peter Williamson, before all the Court of Sessions and before all the lords in Edinburgh, could bring them down that dared put us into slavery!'

'Sh! Dinna trumpet it to the world. You may have the rights of the thing in Edinburgh, but this is not Edinburgh; this is Aberdeen and you have no right to be here, least of all making trouble and stirring up the past.'

'I don't understand what's happened to you! What else are we here for?'

'To move canny and quiet and get away fast. Peter, how able are you for burglary?'

'What do you mean? Breaking and entering?'

'We'll mebbe not have to break in, but entering and taking away ... aye, that is what I have in mind.'

'Man, you're not yourself. What had ye thought to do?'

'You call to mind telling me about the farewell party on board *The Planter*? An' ye recollect a paymaster with a box of cash and a wee book? Well now, this very day I've seen that book and the mannikin that holds it an I tell ye, it's all there! If we could get a look at that wee book it would be all the proof we need.'

'And where would we find it?'

'It's in the office of the Town-Clerk Depute, Walter Cochran. His room is on a small back stair with a door that leads into a close. There are bolts, no locks. I don't know how we would get in, but his door is never closed and I know where he keeps the book, in a wainscot cupboard, with a very simple lock. Could you get us in?'

'No, I could not! I'm not a good man and I've had a wild life, but I am not a criminal! How can we bring the law on these people if we behave like criminals ourselves? You surprise me, James Maclaurin! When we first met you were sore at me because you thought I brought the law into ill repute, and now you suggest that we commit a crime to further our cause.'

'I can think of no other way to get a look at it. I was interrupted by the chief clerk and warned off, otherwise Cochran might even have given it to me in all innocence. Clerk Thomson reminds me of a captured wolf I saw once. He's the one, I'm sure, that wrote the statement they made you sign, and by now he will have set a hunt in motion. If we could only get a good look at the book, enough to make copies, we could get it subpoenaed and put into evidence. But we must make it part of the case first. I'm afraid to put this in the hands of anyone else. If you won't, then I'll do it alone, but I'll need someone to get the back door open for me.'

'How do you expect me to do that?'

'There's a small, leaded window to one side. It has a metal frame that's warped and doesna' close properly.'

'And you want me to climb through?'

'Aye and open the door from the inside. There's no' but a single bolt holds such a wee door and it's in a dark close, and I could keep cavey for ye. So ye'll do it then?'

'Och weel, I couldna' hae ma' ain fayther rin intae yon tollbooth, could I?'

Peter shifted the surly load from his shoulders as he put on the broadest accent he could muster. 'We'll need tinder and steel, and some fine metal to open the lock on the cupboard, and you'll need to have candles, I suppose, and pen and ink?'

150

'Aye, I'll take care of that.'

'Well, it'd better be worth it.'

'Oh, it'll be worth it all right. I caught a glimpse of it. It'll have names and dates and amounts of money. Your Walter Cochran is a careful book-keeper.'

'And once we've looked at it we put it back?'

'Aye, and then we get the judge to have it called in evidence. And, because it is evidence, they *must* produce it.'

'So when do we do the deed?'

'Are you saddle sore?'

'Me? Never.'

'Tonight then.'

'Tonight.'

Chapter 22

Had it not been for George Mackie's wide acquaintance the two ill-fitted burglars would never have got into the building, let alone got their hands on the 'wee book'. As it was, they were loaned a jemmy and a set of skeleton keys and no questions asked. The whisper of the previous evening's gathering had re-opened lost stories of kidnapping, slavery, Peter Williamson's performance and the burning of his book – enough to raise a whole posse of willing accomplices had they, in their turn, been willing to take anyone with them. Of all those who professed themselves eager to help they took but one. He was known only as Hugh and was employed about the city as rat-catcher, chimney-sweep and night-soil man. He offered to keep a lookout, and his presence in the close was not likely to be questioned by the watch, so they accepted his guardianship, and that of his savage-looking dog, with grace and a bottle of whisky in payment.

The oddly assorted trio set out at a time when Hugh assessed it would attract least attention. He himself carried a collection of traps and bait which he believed might net him a few tails while he was waiting. James and Peter slipped into the close and Peter tried the window. As James had reported it had an iron frame set in the stone surround, which was so distorted that it would neither close nor latch. On the other hand it was so rusted that it was difficult to open. The jemmy left marks which they disguised as best they could by rubbing dirt on the scratches. Peter wriggled himself head first through the hole and found that, the floor inside being considerably higher than the level of the alley, he could stand on his hands whilst he manoeuvred his feet through the opening. Finally he fell, rather than climbed, through. It seemed he was in a closet. He had fallen with the most alarming clatter into a heap of buckets, mops and besoms. 'Sh!' he hissed to himself, in the ridiculous way that the desperate need for silence produces, and tiptoed to the door to let James in. The single bar posed no problem and, once the door was closed after them but not fastened, they lit their lantern and crept upstairs.

Cochran's room stood open, as always. In fact they found that the door would not shut, the hinges hanging crooked and the bottom catching on the floorboards. James went straight to the wainscot cupboard and held the lantern for Peter to try his skill with the skeleton keys. The locksmith who had loaned them to George had suggested what size to try and even showed them how to go about the job by demonstrating on George's cash-box, much to the landlord's pretended annoyance, but Peter found it so difficult to get any response from this cupboard lock that in the end, and in impatience, James took over and opened it first try.

Since it was only that morning that Cochran had taken the book out to show James it was lying conveniently at the top of a pile of papers and rolled vellum documents in the cupboard. The two men took it to the desk and, arranging the lantern so that the light fell on the pages, they began to read.

*

To say that what they found there was exciting would be an understatement. Peter and James read out in intense whispers the names and dates that they found, sometimes reading the same entry, sometimes overlapping each other, sometimes interrupting.

'To Colonel Horsie who sells his concubine, one guinea!'

'To Robert Ross for his son, one shilling.'

'To John Smith, one shilling cash spent with three whores at The Windmill. To look at him you'd never suspect it.'

'Would you put that on your expense account with the Crosbies?'

'To Helen Law for boarding servants, ten pence per day.'

'To John Smith for bringing in boys, three shillings... Ah, here! Listen to this: January 17th 1743, one shilling and sixpence to the man who brought in Peter Williamson! Turn over, turn over ... and here, look! January 8th, to one pair stockings to Peter Williamson, sixpence ... and here: to five days' board of Williamson, one shilling and threepence!'

'To making two shirts to Williamson, fourpence. You did well out of them for clothes.'

'Aye, but you know what this means? It proves everything. They can't say I wasn't there; they can't say I was lying!'

'Very well then, let's copy it all out. I'll get the total too and the first and last dates. Look at the fly-leaf, Peter. Look at the names there. Baillie William Fordyce and company and John Smith. Fordyce was one of the names on *The Planter*'s contract. And he's a baillie, and a J.P., and God knows what all! Oh Peter, Peter my son, we've got them cold!'

'Hold on a wee while. I'm still getting the drift. There's much more to this than I thought. These douce citizens whose names are on the fly-leaf of this book are the same men that had me lifted from the streets, and you say that this Fordyce is a baillie, that would have signed the papers that had us sold overseas? The same men that owned the ship had us poor children taken up? It's hard to credit, James. The same men ...'

'Aye, well, that's what I was saying earlier. It explains why they were so keen to get you off the public highway with your Indian dress and the crowds you were drawing by telling the tale. If there'd been anyone by to put two and two together they'd have been discredited and totally put to shame. No wonder they rushed you into recanting, and themselves into burning the evidence. Now let's copy this down and away before Hugh gets restless.'

They copied furiously.

They heard the dog's bark in a panic, for it seemed as though he was on the stairs. This had been a signal arranged between the three of them for a state of alarm, and yet, although it took a deal longer than a minute to return the book and to re-lock the cupboard door, not to have locked it would have been a fatal mistake. So they pretended a calmness they did not feel, put everything back as they had found it, even scraping a spatter of candlewax off the desk, and crept out of the room. There was no sign of the dog on the stairs, but they stood for a moment, listening by the open back door, ready to scurry into the closet if need be. They could hear no voices, nothing to indicate trouble. On the other hand, Hugh might have been taken away. Then they heard his blessed voice, close to the door.

154

'Are ye there? 'Twas a wee moosie the cur was chasin', ran below the door. It's all clear and nae a body in the streets. Ye can come out now and no hindrance.'

James opened the door further, to allow himself to slip into the close, while Peter fastened it behind him and made a clumsy exit from the closet window. This time he climbed up and came out feet first, which caused some deep growling from the dog but which brought him safe into company with the others.

'I'll about my business, gentleman,' said Hugh, grinning. 'Unless either of yous would come along? There's more privy deeds to be done, the nicht!'

They could not prevent him roaring his way down the street in laughter, while James shook his head at the awfulness of the pun.

'We should never have given him the whisky!'

'No one will pay him the least mind, the state he's in, and he's done us proud. Let's away, for we've an early start in the morning.'

They had arranged with George Mackie that, if all went well, they would leave at first light so as not to bring any trouble to him. He had protested his willingness to hide them from the law if necessary, but James had assured him that they had achieved all that anyone could want and that the copy of the book was worth a thousand further witnesses.

So it was that they packed their bags and left, prosaically, on the coach. Anybody watching the departure of the daily stage would tell the authorities that they had gone, looking downcast and with no-one to see them off.

Chapter 23

During the whole of the long, cold and tedious journey back to Edinburgh the two men perforce spoke little. Even during the overnight stops they shared nothing of significance. Peter had wanted to find out more about the evidence that James had collected and to expound upon his own significant finds, but in the public atmosphere of the coach journey there was little opportunity for quiet conversation, and they were still wary of being tracked down by Thomson or his men. Peter's black-dog mood returned gradually, born out of the rejection he felt, or imagined, and intensified by James' sleepy abstraction. The old law clerk was sifting through the evidence of others almost as though he were reading it page by page, and, in this manner, he would sometimes go back and replay some scene in his mind or dwell on some line of testimony that seemed to him significant. In that secret recess in his consciousness there was no place for Peter.

Peter was usually the first to climb aboard the stage and, taking a corner seat in tense ill humour, would stare out of the window hour after hour. The other travellers, climbing and descending, making shorter journeys, busy and chatting, would stare at the hunched figure with pity, as if at a bereavement and, shaking their heads at each other, hastily look away. He who had been the survivor of so much and seen so much, had had a window opened for a moment by what had happened in Aberdeen, and all his susceptibilities set raw and hopeful. Now, instead of running back for a fresh jump at life, he had to remain silent. His wounds were covered up again, his story and his action taken over and bandaged with the confusion of other griefs and other stories... 'To Robert Ross for inlisting his son, one shilling...' Oh, Robert, what ailed ye, to sell the boy to slavery for a shilling? And Jamie, poor Jamie, beating the drum, with the tears coursing down his cheeks, taken naked in sleep from the foot of his parents' bed; could the people not keep their children safe? The public injustice meted out to him had become the people's cause, and he had no special ownership of it. The private revenge that he had fought for had become a public scandal, taken out of his hands by a faded law-clerk. Indian Peter was no longer a solo performance; other hands than his had written the story and leading rôles had been given to other actors. His misery was compounded by the knowledge that this jealousy was demeaning. He knew that he was not the only one who had suffered, but he had learned to come to terms with his own injury, even to enjoy the power it gave him to affect others. Now he was being asked to take responsibility for more than his own past suffering, and he did not know that he could. James was no help. He would tell him nothing. Their relationship had come to an end; Peter had become just a sworn fact in a case at law, to be put into the third person and stripped of feeling. There was no way to recapture the past few days.

Walking on the banks of Loch Leven while changing horses, James, who was only too well aware of Peter's blackness but could not break through to him, tried to find some spark of illumination for the future.

'We'll be on the ferry tomorrow. Will you go straight home?'

'Oh aye, if I can be sure where home is.'

'What will your wife have been doing while you were away?'

Peter looked at him very oddly. There was a hint of the old devil for a moment, before James apologized and rephrased his question. 'Will she be staying with family or will she be running the shop?'

'The "shop" is rather beneath my wife's dignity, ye ken. I am also beneath my wife's dignity, but ... I shall go home ... to my wife. Once before, when I went home to "my wife", her father barred the door to me. That time she was dead, and my only child was dead. This time, who knows?'

'I'm sorry.'

James was at a loss with this man. The undue stress he placed on 'my wife' did not seem so much sarcasm as mockery of James himself. But then Peter took his arm and shook him a little.

'Why do you not come with me? Eh, Father? I'll dare swear she's gone to her father, that keeps a bookshop. He doesna' care overmuch for me, but he maintains a good cellar and good books. Ye'd be much of an age, I'm thinking, and I'll be sworn ye've neither fire nor food to your rooms? What do you say? Will you protect me from my in-laws?'

'I was wondering if ye'd come back with me. Since we've shared so many beds the last two-three weeks, it'd seem friendly. And there's things we should discuss to get this case under way.'

'I should go home, don't you think?'

'Aye, mebbe.'

'And ye'll come alsweel.'

'Very well, if ye're sure.'

So, once more, the moment passed. By bringing them closer together, but making sure that they would still not be alone, Peter had contrived that there was no opportunity for clearing the air, nor purging his jealousy.

'We'll be sure to drop this pretence that I'm your father, will we not? Your family knows about the law-suit? I know your wife does, for she said so when she took the money at your performance.'

'Yes, we'll drop the pretence and come clean. The circus is over for a season and we can all go back to normal. You can juggle the evidence and I'll jump through the hoop for everybody's entertainment.'

And then the horn sounded, and the coach lumbered on towards Dunfermline and the Queen's Ferry.

*

The next few weeks were ones of feverish activity. James had scarce time to open up his rooms or get the bedding aired before he was summoned to long hours at the law office. They had to find him a desk there, like old times, and he and Andrew pored over the depositions day after day. They had no time to bother about Peter. He came when asked, he brought his baptismal record, he verified the details of his arrest and the burning of his books, he was sworn into secrecy about the methods they had taken to see Cochran's 'wee book' – and he was abandoned.

He gave no more performances in his howff; he spent little enough time at home. He took to having himself carried in a sedan chair through the streets in full Indian rig, and he sat for a statue, carved in wood, which was to be placed in the Cannonmills. Some days he took off, and was to be seen skimming stones with the children on the foreshore, or holed up in some sailor's tavern in Leith where he would be drunk for days. It was in just such company that he was tracked down by a freckled lad with a message from Andrew.

'He says ye're to spruce yersel' an get down to his office... At once! An' he says if ye're no sober I'm tae pit ye un'er the pump.'

'Oh, so I'm wanted, am I? Well now, isn't that just fine! You can tak' yersen back to your maister an' tell him I'm well eneugh where I am, an I'll come when I've a mind to and no' a moment afore.'

The men he was with all applauded, but they soon saw to it that he was propped up and sobered down and parcelled into a hired gig. The boy rode on the back and whistled and hollered so loud that folk turned their heads to see who it was, rattling by. He dropped off as they neared the law office and Peter was left to pay the gig and to stroll as calmly as he could through the lobby. The old, peeling doorkeeper left him outside while he announced him, and Peter caught a look at himself in the dark glass of the door. What difference did it make what he looked like? Did they want to parade him before the Lord Ordinary like a beast at a show? Was it not enough that the lawyers and judges put on fine clothes and spoke fine words? Nevertheless, he slicked back his hair the best he could and straightened his cravat.

'Peter, sit you down! Well man, the time has come!'

Nothing about neglect, nothing about how sorry we are to have forgotten all about you. Not even criticism of his behaviour. Like a spoilt child, Peter thought he would have preferred a scolding to being ignored altogether. Andrew leaned across the desk, his hands clasped so tight in excitement that the knuckles showed white.

'Lord Minto has set a day to hear the pleas in law.'

'When is that?'

'The fifth of February.'

'That's the day after tomorrow.'

'Aye, I know, but we're ready. There's nothing now remains to be done.'

'But I've no idea what I'm supposed to do! Ye've told me nothing, nor prepared me for what will happen. Do you not think I have a right to be told?'

'Oh, you've no need to fret. It'll all go through on a by-blow. There's no need for you to be at the court at all. I only thought you might be interested.'

For a moment Peter could neither breathe nor move. He was drowning, over and over again. A suspended moment, which felt like an hour, hung between the two men, until the hot blood rushed to his face and the pent up anger of weeks burst out of him.

'Man alive! Might be interested? Who do you think I am? Am I some bag of old papers to be used and thrown aside? Who is bringing this charge? Who has right and a claim to this justice? And who do you think has been injured enough and hurt enough and yet done your dirty work and put his head in the noose and found your evidence and... Whose case is it, for God's sake? Did I go through all that, just so's you could make a name for yourself? Interested! I'd say, I am ... likely ... to be interested!'

'Mister Williamson! Mister Williamson, I'm sorry. I thought, with having an establishment in the Luckenbooths, so close – almost in the courthouse – you'd be more familiar with how the law works. I should have thought ... I'm really sorry. Let me explain...'

'Oh, don't put yourself about on my account. I understand that this is now your case. I can see it here!' He pulled out a sheaf of paper, and proceeded to read aloud the finely written words that headed it.

' "Poor Peter Williamson, late of the Province of Pennsylvania in North America, Planter, now residenter in Edinburgh, Pursuer, against Alexander Cushnie late Dean of Guild and Procurator-Fiscal of the Borough Court of Aberdeen, and others: Defenders!" So "poor" Peter Williamson is the pursuer. But, as he has never even heard of the rabbit he's pursuing, nor is to be allowed into the court, how could he possibly have any further interest in the pursuit?'

He flung himself out of the room and out of the building. He tore blindly out of the city, from the cold reek of the smoke-laden fog into the frozen mist of the hills beyond, until he could go no further. He had no idea where he was and he had no idea where he was going, or whether he was going anywhere at all. He stood at a gate, letting the cold damp soak into the burning rage of his resentment.

There was no reason in this world why he should not get himself into the court. There were so many friends – or at least so many men who owed him a favour and who used his coffee shop in the Luckenbooths as a place for quiet, legal conspiracy, who would lend him a gown, or smuggle him in as a clerk. But it was the principle that irked him, if he thought clearly at all. He should have known that the practice of the law is constructed deliberately to de-personalize, and defuse anger and revenge. But he was not thinking clearly; he was full of the same cancer of injustice that had driven him in the barn in Aberdeen and in the mountains of Appalachia, and had refused James into his life on the shores of Lake Leven. Without any idea of where he was, or where he was going, he heaved himself away from the gate and lurched on.

There was nothing in field or hedge to feed a man in the wild hills and he had no money but a few pieces of small silver. He took himself a stem of blackthorn from where the hedger had left it and whittled it into a staff; he accepted a lift on a carrier's cart, with a tale of looking for work, and he made a hungry pilgrimage south. It was hunger that, in the end, brought him to the players.

They were on a circuit that took them to York for the end of Lent, but this was a lean time, of barn-storming and the weekly fairs and markets. They may have called themselves players, but others would have driven them from the door as 'rogues, vagabonds, Egyptians, thiggers and sorners'. It sounded a matter of pride to these men and women to have such titles, even though they may have had no more understanding than Peter of what they meant. They came from throughout Europe: jugglers, acrobats, rope dancers, fortune-tellers and tricksters. They displayed the story of Judith and Holophernes with a deal of horses' blood begged from the knackers, and they took Indian Peter to their hearts. They found him a clever boy who soon learnt the drum beats, and they teamed him up with a woman fire-eater. He could never say her name and she spoke some Cracovian tongue but, dressed in skins and feathers, she played her torches over Peter's scarred body in a ritual of torture, delighting the crowds several times a day.

Sometimes the drumming and the smoke caused her to become careless and Peter took some hurt which in the reality of his rôle, he could not cry against. Sometimes he himself did not notice the burns until later, but always the small pain of the blistered flesh burnt away a little of the larger pain of his anger.

Through all the border country into England Indian Peter drew audiences. Never large groups, for the country was sparse and the season early. It was the heavy smell of the gorse and the lambs crying that turned the company towards York and Peter north again, towards home. They would pick up their over-wintering, outdoor acts, the animals and the heavy equipment of the flying chairs. Peter, his fierce energy run down, would pick up his old life again. He knew that whatever performance he had given with the travellers, another and more elaborate show had been given in the courtroom in his absence.

What had passed while he was away was the slow pageant of the law's majesty. James had sought him high and low; the gangs of small boys had failed to bring him in. Andrew, however, had gone ahead, caught up in the momentum of the hearings and petitions and counter petitions that put him to his first real test. James sat with him through it all, a huge paternal pride swelling his chest as this son of his old master strung argument and language together before the law lords of Scotland.

First came the pleas in law, remarkable in that what was being charged brought the law against the law.

'For having,' said Andrew, 'acknowledged that they ordered a prosecution against the pursuer, before their baillie-court, at the instance of their Dean of Guild, who acts constantly as Procurator-Fiscal of that court; it is evident, therefore, whence this complaint took its rise, that is from the magistrates themselves, and consequently they are answerable, not only for their judicial actings as judges of the court to whom it was presented, but as private parties, for anything calumnious or ill-grounded that may be found in the complaint itself. The notoriety of the practice mentioned in the Pursuer's pamphlet leaves no room for doubt that the magistrates were conscious of the truth of these facts; their reason, therefore, of endeavouring to suppress this pamphlet, or discrediting its authority, could not proceed from a zeal for truth and for the character of the town and community of Aberdeen, but must be owing to some other motive which, though it may be guessed at, yet as there is no direct evidence of it in process, the Pursuer will

162

not attempt to point it out; it is sufficient for him to show that the proceedings of the magistrates were irregular and oppressive, abstracting from any interested motive they may have had in this prosecution.'

'A Daniel come to judgement! Yea, a Daniel! Oh wise young judge, how I do honour thee!'

James had never seen *The Merchant of Venice* nor even read the play, but these lines came into his head and stuck there like a chant. Plant a doubt about the motives of the accused and then go on to claim that they are not competent to try a complaint that they themselves have brought! Then, oh my Lord, go for the kill, by saying that, even if their case against Peter was a proper one and they the proper court to have tried it, nevertheless, they had allowed him no time to find his defence and in truth coerced him into signing a retraction! A Daniel, a very Daniel!

What James admired above all else was the weaving into the fabric of his plea the bright threads of another yarn. Andrew laid these threads out with extreme delicacy, and yet they shone through like gold. Not only did he contest the points of law upon which he begged the Lord Ordinary to find the magistrates guilty, but he wove a tissue of suggestion that, far from having burnt a scandalous pamphlet full of calumnies and lies, the baillies had rushed Peter into denying what was true and could be proved. He nudged the Court of Session into awareness that there was a good deal more than a legal principle here, and asked to be able to present proof.

Lord Minto, Ordinary, allowed himself an avuncular and smiling patronage when giving his finding that, in law, Peter was liable for damages against the magistrates, just as Andrew was smiling like a Cheshire cat when his Lordship also allowed Proof. But first there had to be an opportunity for the Defenders to appeal. Both James and Andrew were surprised when, in fact, they did just that. They had thought that they would prefer to pay the damages, and keep the whole thing quiet. Perhaps, following Peter and James' visit to Aberdeen, the news had already got about, perhaps they felt so aggrieved at the man's success, or perhaps their guilt weighed heavy, but, whatever the reason, the Aberdeen magistrates appealed against the decision in the Inner Court on February 4th, 1762, two days after Lord Minto's interlocutor. The Crosbies were very aware that the present court session would have come to an end on March 12th, and there would be the familiar delays before any appeal would be finally considered.

'Would you listen to this?' shouted Andrew in his father's room, as James presented him with the papers from Aberdeen. 'They say they've been misunderstood.'

The two older men tried to hush him, but he was too excited for that.

'They claim to have no knowledge of any slave trade, any kidnapping, or any indentures wrongly attested. They've never heard of Mr Cochran's wee book, and Williamson's book they consider a calumnious aspersion on the merchants of Aberdeen ... while Williamson, they say ... Och it's as well he's not here to hear this, James ... Williamson's an "idle stroller who could give no good account of himself and had produced this pamphlet to be composed for him, of such shocking circumstances in order the more easily to impose upon and draw money from the incredulous vulgar." And finally they go on to say that they could not have been prejudiced against Peter since they had never seen him before, and sinned through ignorance and not through any sinister design; therefore, they are innocent.'

'Sounds like panic to me, son. And they've laid a trap for themselves where you've just to give them a wee push and they'll be in it heels over hurdle.'

'What's that then, father?'

'Why, they've defended themselves on the ground of ignorance, yet Cochran is Clerk of the court and, so James tells us, one of the owners of *The Planter*. And is not Baillie William Fordyce, in whose court Peter was made to recant, the chief owner of the ship? As James can prove that fact, even without Williamson's testimony, you should get this thrown out by their lordships without any trouble. But, anyway, you're sure to find a good many other windows wide open. If their lordships adhere to the Lord Ordinary's interlocutor you need go no further, but if you want to go on with this and offer proof then he has allowed you to do so, just as the magistrates will also be allowed proof in reply. In fact, they are asking for trouble because they have said that his book is full of fancies and untruths, so they are laying themselves open for proof to be brought either way.'

'We'll need Peter for that, won't we? I wish he'd not run off that day. What would they say if they knew that he'd gone missing again? Surely they'd make much of the fact?'

'Of a certainty they would. You should never have let him alone so long. But you know that now. They'll say he was lying, they'll say he could not go through with it, they'll say it proves that he is an idle, strolling mischief-maker, and the only hope you've got is that the proof is always submitted in the first instance in writing. If the Inner Court takes its time to consider the appeal and the Aberdeen magistrates ask for time to assemble their evidence, then we've got time to find Indian Peter and bring him into the limelight.'

In the event they did not need to find him. In the fullness of time, the Inner Court upheld the Lord Ordinary's interlocutor and allowed both parties proof, James and Andrew submitted their written record with abstracts of all the depositions, and the session came to an end on March the twelfth without any decision having been reached.

Chapter 24

Once his first anger and impatience with Peter was over, James had thought long and hard about him. He had been at some pains to try to get Andrew to understand and not to write him off, or to take undue blame for his disappearance.

'He's a survivor. He's scarred in mind and body, but he's come through worse than this since his mother died when he was a bairn. The scars have hardened and there's not much soft kindness left in the man, and not much room for sympathy, or understanding, or any compassion. He'll be a rotten husband to that wife of his, I'm thinking, and you'd best put no reliance on him, Mister Andrew.'

'I thought you'd changed your opinion of him, James.'

'I have. I feel towards the rascal like he was my own son. But that's no' to say I cannot see his faults, nor that he can help driving me to distraction. He's my prodigal and you're my pride and joy, and I want for the two of you the best that life can offer.'

'Then we'd best put all we can into winning this case for him, "in absentia" as it were.'

When the Court rose after the Easter recess Andrew's proof was delivered with all the power of his own need for achievement and a masterly production it turned out to be.

The record was then closed and the lords sat in consideration.

*

And then, one day, Peter strolled in to the Crosbies' office, confident, unabashed and as thin as a rake.

'I've made my peace with Mary and with mysen'. Do you want that I should kneel to you too?'

What could they say? They were no longer angry, nor even unduly curious. They were held in limbo, waiting for the decision of the

166

Inner Court, and with other cases on the books and other witnesses to interview. In Purgatory there is neither condemnation nor forgiveness.

James was laid off once more. The Crosbies offered him work, but he knew that it was only a sinecure, and that there would be resentment among the other clerks at his reinstatement; besides, the desk space that he would take up was badly needed in such cramped accommodation. There was another reason too why he turned down their offer. He wanted to keep an eye on Peter. 'Oh, not spying, you understand,' he said to Andrew, and repeated often to himself in reassurance, 'not spying at all. It's just that the man is troubled, and I would like to be at hand if he takes it into his head to flit again.'

Peter, however, showed no sign of flitting. His howff always closed down at the end of session, and since he had been missing for some considerable time business had not been good. He renewed the lease on the building and scrubbed and cleaned and painted. He threw out some of the old benches in favour of chairs, and rearranged tables until the place had a fresh, clean look that was far from the greasy drinking shop it had been before. His intention was to turn it into a coffee shop with news sheets tied to polished wooden poles: a place where not only the dirt court lawyers, but poets, writers and judges could happily meet their acquaintance. A notice was displayed on the door that orders might be placed there for the attention of his wife, who was setting up as a mantua maker, and his father-in-law had placed books on the shelves besides the china pitchers that were known as pigs. Instead of the checked tablecloths, Mary made plain white linen cloths and Peter intended to serve wine and sweet biscuits to his new, and (he hoped) more elegant clientele. James came over most days and the two men talked about the future. Peter was frenetically full of plans. He was developing the idea of running a penny post, inspired by the letter-carrying system he had seen operating so well up and down the Delaware. He talked enthusiastically about making a street directory of Edinburgh, of setting up his own printing press, and of publishing his books again, now that the case was so nearly over and the ban about to be lifted. He drafted announcements to be placed in all the news sheets in the north of England, as well as Scotland, and could scarcely contain his impatience for the final judgement.

James tried to cool his certainty without destroying the confidence that kept the man within sight and working. He was never sure, as he watched him scrambling through the chaos of his reconstruction, whether the activity was, in truth, confidence or a blanking out of doubt, but he understood the need for achievement and the panacea of physical labour. He was also very aware that Peter was getting himself deeper and deeper into debt and would need every penny of compensation that the court might give.

The session rose and the coffee shop opened. There were a number of clubs and meeting places in Edinburgh and the unscheduled timing of the courts' day-to-day activity made a place to meet almost a necessity. Business was brisk and Peter began to make money. James acted as an unofficial host, and sometimes as an extra pair of hands waiting at table ... 'not spying, you understand.'

When the Inner Court heard the appeal by the magistrates against Lord Minto's interlocutor, Peter was not only briefed but, surrounded as he was by the life of the courts, he was tuned in to the ritual once more and accepted the rules of conduct quite freely. Andrew took him through the answers he intended offering to refute the Aberdeen magistrates. The high tone of the words produced a glow that seemed to light up the lawyer's chambers as the young advocate rehearsed his part. Peter and James took over the rôle of their lordships and quietly listened as the dusk grew in the corners.

'Liberty is a balance between the rights of the people and the authority of magistrates; therefore, it is a point of public welfare if complaints are brought against magistrates and can be proved. Since your lordships have accepted Peter Williamson's proof as substantiating the truth of his story, the magistrates have now changed their plea to one of ignorance at the time of his arrest... Not that they were justified in their actions but that they did not realize that he was telling the truth!

'But, your Lordships, they must have known, because selling boys was done openly. Parties of men, like press-gangs, were employed publicly in patrolling the streets of Aberdeen and seizing by force such boys as seemed proper subjects of the slave trade.

'It is in vain that the petitioners represent the events of Williamson's arrest as improbable and claim that he has slandered them in this and

168

the whole question of their involvement with the kidnapping, since a gentleman of great worth and integrity was at that time at the head of the magistracy, the Provost of Aberdeen. There is no doubt that he did intervene in cases of extreme violence, as in the deposition of Margaret Ross, but only after private entreaty and advice and not with the power of his office in law. This, my Lords, suggests that he could not act against the inclination and interest of his colleagues.'

'In other words, they're all in it together, which is what you said all along, James!' interrupted Peter. Andrew held up his hand, smiling, for silence and continued.

'Not only are the merchants, no fewer than fifteen, featured in this trade, but magistrates are also implicated, not only by general opinion but also by witness of the names mentioned in the Birth Brieves as having ownership of *The Planter*, those of Baillie William Fordyce and his partners. No fewer than sixty-nine boys and girls can be proved to his account from Walter Cochran's book.

'My Lords, how is it possible that a full bench of six magistrates can forget what happened fourteen years before? Nor is it reasonable that they alone have remained ignorant when everyone else knew what was going on. It was magistrates who brought the complaint against Peter Williamson in the first place. You should ask yourselves, "Why?", my Lords.' Peter and James chorused 'Why?', no longer being able to contain their exuberance. Peter reached to the floor and picked up a duster. He draped it over his head and peered with pretended short-sightedness at Andrew. The advocate could not keep a straight face but rushed through the rest of his submission.

'Why? It proves that they were uneasy about it. There was no notice given; it was summary justice; threatening, and wrongful imprisonment; and in bringing any action against Williamson they become private parties and, as such, have no special powers. If they bring a case of slander it is because they are injured parties, which proves that they were involved! THEY ARE NOT ABOVE THE LAW!'

Andrew was dancing about the room with a chair as his partner. Peter and James both hiccupped with laughter as Crosbie senior, coming back into chambers after hours, to see what they were up to, peeped round the door at all the hullabaloo.

'Peter Williamson,' thundered Andrew, unaware of his father's presence, 'is likely to be branded a vagrant for ever and stripped of his livelihood, for he now has the character of a lying imposter...'

'Thank you very much.'

Peter rose and bowed deeply so that the duster fell from his head. Straightening up, he caught sight of Alexander Crosbie, as did the other two and, like guilty children in school, they were quick to apologize.

'Dinna fash yersels! Will they uphold the Lord Ordinary, do you think?'

'No doubt. No doubt at all.' James came to his old master and shook him by the hand. 'Yon clown advocate will be a judge himself afore long, even if you and I never live to see it. It's a fine piece of advocacy and he'll do you proud. Don't scold the lad for his high spirits. It's just nervousness, and better here than in court.'

'Are you happy about it, Peter?' Andrew was serious now.

'Oh aye, it'll do me fine! If'n we come away with the prize, what follows?'

'Will both parties be allowed proof?' Mister Crosbie was setting the furniture to rights and tidying up.

'Proof has been submitted and is on record, but the appeal had to be heard first. Surely they will drop the whole thing now? If the Lord Ordinary's interlocutor holds it would be expensive to carry on, perhaps to the next session, just to hear evidence.'

'I agree, but then we did not reckon on them appealing the first time. They can still challenge Peter's evidence, bring their own witnesses or contest the amount of damages. What are you asking?'

'One hundred pounds in compensation and twenty-three pounds seven shillings expenses.'

'If it is a question of evidence, or settling sums of money, they will either have to go back to the outer court, probably before Lord Minto – which they may not wish to do, knowing how he feels about the case so far – or they will have to go to some other body.'

'Such as what? What body?'

'A local court, perhaps.'

'They'd never do that, surely?'

'I'd think it unlikely that they would want the publicity.'

'Could I force them to a local court?' Peter took the lawyers by surprise.

'Why? You'd put your case back before the same magistrates that jailed you! Knowing what you know about them, do you think you'd get a fair hearing?'

'I think the people of Aberdeen would get a fair hearing.'

'Peter ... Tak' tent.'

'James, you above all know what I mean. At one time I resented that others were involved. It muddied the waters. But I'm clearer in my mind now. I'll not only take care for myself but I owe it to the others to have this out in the open. Your Edinburgh courts have done me fine. How could it have been otherwise, with me a carline rogue banished my own town? I could never get justice then. But now, if they've been ordered to face my charges and hear my evidence, and if ... oh, I know well it is still "if" ... If'n the Inner Court tells them they have to pay heed to me, how can they do other than all according to the books? The people of Aberdeen will have a chance to come into court and have their say, and it'll not all be out of the way here, with evidence on paper and the judges reading it all at home by their own fires!'

James drew him aside. 'Peter, son, you're forgetting something. How will you pay for all this? These good men have done all and more to help you to justice, but how can they go on when you've no' but two bawbees in your pocket?'

Peter thought it through and then turned back to the lawyers. 'If the magistrates refuse to accept the Inner Court and want to go on with the evidence, then surely they must pay to continue?'

'Ay, there's something in what you say, but you are still the pursuer and it will cost you something.' Crosbie had put the shutters across the windows and was ready to take his son home. 'And this after-hours consultation will also go on your bill if we continue beyond supper time. Let's wait until we see how Andrew makes out with their lordships before we plan further.'

*

The decision to uphold the Lord Ordinary's interlocutor was delivered, signed and sealed, but wrapped in an extraordinary legal package:

evidence on both sides could be heard and there was a case to be answered; but, when the matter of compensation arose, it was suggested that the parties elect to go to arbitration. Andrew was astounded.

'I had no idea, did you Father, that an important case like this could be decided upon by an arbiter?'

'There's no reason at all, in law, why not. Admittedly arbitration is usually for small matters of dispute, of which your damages might be part, but I can see why Aberdeen would agree. It's less expensive … much less expensive; it's also quicker, since they do not have to abide by the sessions of the courts and – and this is maybe why they have agreed to it – the hearing is in private.'

'Peter won't like that. Who appoints the arbiter?'

'That is a matter for mutual agreement. An arbiter in a land dispute might be a surveyor, but I'm thinking they'll have to find an advocate, someone qualified and skilled in law for this case. I'm saying, "they", because it would be best to have one for Peter and one for the magistrates and an oversman to whom they can refer if necessary.'

Peter was not cast down by the news. 'It'll not be private for long. If I win, I'll publish. They'll not be able to stop me. It'll make people sit up and listen if I print an account of the whole sorry business. And I'll make sure they hear everything; everyone who has a story to tell will stand before the men who wronged them and they'll be forced to hear it.'

'It may not work out like that, Peter. Only the arbiter will have to be there, but there will be evidence and cross examination. It will not be as formal as in a court but there will be much the same rules governing evidence, and they will be bound by the same oath as if they were in court.'

With many apologies, to the Crosbies and to James, Peter withdrew all the depositions, all the documents and Cochran's wee book, and got the court's permission to use them again.

'I'll do this on my own, Andrew. I'm wiser now. You and your father, and most especially James, have taught me so much that I can never repay. I'll get the money I owe you, but the rest … see how I do, first, and if I don't let you down … that's one advantage of arbitration: I can make my own mistakes.'

'If you don't insist we go by sea, I'll come with you.'

Peter stared at James in surprise. 'Into the lion's den? After Cochran's office?'

'I've nothing to do here, and some savings over the last months. Let me be your father, in law!'

They laughed over the ridiculous pun and that was how it was settled. James made a sedate way north, arriving well before November 3rd, the date set for the commencement of the process, which had to be completed before November 15th, and Peter, having arranged for the management of his affairs with his real father-in-law, followed hot-foot after.

Chapter 25

The informality of the arbitration was in evidence from the beginning. The proceedings were delayed for a day while John Thain, who was Peter's 'doer' buried his mother-in-law. But on November 4th the two Aberdonian advocates, John Thain and James Petrie, 'doer' for the defenders, sat in a draughty meeting-hall on hard wooden benches to hear the evidence. There was a sour smell of recently washed wood and never-opened windows, and none of the visual ceremony of the Court of Sessions; there was a kind of solemnity, nevertheless, with the swearing in of witnesses and the formality of the examination of their statements.

At first it looked as though, ranged against the devastating combination of advocates to arbitrate, and magistrates, sheriffs and clerks of the courts as defenders, Peter would be at a disadvantage, with only a retired law-clerk at his side. He was panicked several times into playing ridiculous legal games, trying to trap the well-rehearsed witnesses called by the defenders, who, themselves, more than once said that they had other things to do and please would he get on with it. On the whole, however, the smattering of legal mumbo-jumbo he had picked up in the Luckenbooths in Edinburgh stood him in good stead and proceedings went very generally according to the ordered conduct of the law.

James felt the cold, but sat, wrapped in rugs with a charcoal warmer to his feet. With mittened fingers he made notes, or held whispered conferences with Peter. The arbiters frequently adjourned sessions in order for the whole company to warm themselves and get food and drink from the nearest hostelry.

The names and charges were different now. Instead of a case for wrongful arrest the interest had shifted to what was contained in Peter's book. If he could not prove that what he wrote there was true, then the magistrates were right. They, and the merchants, had been slandered, and were entirely justified in what they had already done to Peter, even if they had not used the right way of going about it. So the names that appeared on the indictment were those of 'Captain' – not Baillie – William Fordyce of Aquhorties; Walter Cochran of Dumbreck and portioner of Ferryhill, Town Clerk Depute of Aberdeen; Patrick Barron of Woodside and company; and Alexander Mitchell. Many of those who had had shares in *The Planter*, or who had been employed by them, were already dead, so the list was short. After some time spent in eliminating Patrick Barron, who insisted on coming and repeating what he had already told James, that he was a carpenter, and was not, nor ever had been, a dealer in servants, the real business began.

The owners of *The Planter* and those who had worked for them in taking servants were effectively on trial. If it was a campaign against slavery, then Peter had already won the first round, simply by having the case heard.

James was not sure about Peter's motives, just as he could not be sure about his own. The law sometimes makes a clear injustice obscure, so that what is being tried has little or nothing to do with the grievance.

Was Peter lying? The law existed to examine that issue and that alone. Would any amount of evidence prove that slavery was a criminal offence, or even morally wrong?

Arbitration cannot examine criminal cases, yet the arbiters would have to hear evidence of slavery. None of that evidence could be used in drawing up a case against that practice, but it could be stated on the floor and go into the record, and perhaps turn up again, hundreds of years later. Those who thought that slavery was something that happened only to black people might be taken aback when they heard that it was commonplace among white people too. Oppression is no accounter of race or time.

The arbiters first heard the plain facts of the ownership of *The Planter*, of how Captain Ragg bought her from London as *The Kenilworth* and how she was renamed. They were told that it was intended to bring back a cargo of tobacco; of the shares taken by merchants, most of whom were known to each other; of the appointment of James Smith to engage and indent as many servants as he could procure to go along with *The Planter*. In plain, factual language they heard the story of how the ship, in her passage to America, was wrecked upon an island near Cape May and entirely lost, but that the crew and passengers were saved; that such of the passengers and servants as Robert Ragg could get after the wreck were carried to Philadelphia and there sold. Nobody could say that the defenders were not honest people, nor that they were witholding evidence or hiding anything.

The arbiters were pleased. Everything seemed tidy and devoid of drama. Peter had submitted a mountain of paper from the previous hearing at the Court of Sessions but they had the abstract made by James Maclaurin and Andrew Crosbie to help find their way through it. Peter had also added some further evidence taken from sailors in Edinburgh, which had been sealed up by the court and delivered under that seal to the arbiters. They could have been forgiven for a degree of complacency and self importance in receiving such a commission. It was certainly a far more important case than the usual arbitration over land claims or disputed wills. It had sounded like a simple matter of how much compensation Peter would get for the loss of his books and reputation, after the mess the magistrates had made of getting him locked up without due notice.

*

The first to be called was Robert Thomson, the Town Clerk. He was a busy man with little enough time to waste on such matters as claims for compensation, so he asked to go first. He gave his evidence, cold and clear, with no sign of recognizing James, nor of the vicious anger that he had shown when he found him intruding in Cochran's office. James had tried to convince Peter of the fear this man had aroused in him but now he sat and watched as the two men, Williamson and Thomson, played canny, skirting politely round each other like fighting bull terriers – no snapping and snarling, only bared teeth and terrible smiles.

'About, or rather previous to the time libelled, I remember that it was a practice among some of the merchants in Aberdeen of indenting servants to go for America. I know nothing of any such merchants being employed, or employing others, in kidnapping boys or girls

176

under age; neither did I ever see any indented servant attested by a magistrate or inferior judge but who appeared to be past the age of pupillarity and who judicially declared that they had signed their indentures willingly.'

He had it all written down. Prompting himself from the script in his hand he went on. 'I never saw any persons under confinement, except that I remember once, in the street called the Green, I saw a parcel of people in a barn, and heard them merry, and a piper along with them. And having asked what they were, I was told they were indented servants for America. I remember the doors of the barn were open and people standing in them.'

His answers to any question were snappish and brief. No, he never saw any list of servants. No, he never kept any such list. The indentures were attested by a magistrate and immediately carried off by the owner thereof. On being shown Cochran's account book, however, the smile – or rictus – that displayed sharp canine teeth was directed straight at James.

'Indeed, I have seen this book before. I saw it produced by Mister Cochran, my Clerk Depute, when it was demanded in the process between the said Peter Williamson and the magistrates of Aberdeen.'

Peter asked him to look at the last page of the book and he did so. There was no change in his expression at all.

'Do you see the date, April the twenty-third?'

'Yes.'

'Do you see an article charged therein: Cash from Mister Thomson, ten pounds sterling?'

'Yes.'

'Did you pay that sum to James Smith?'

'I remember nothing of paying such a sum. Nor do I believe I am the Mister Thomson therein mentioned.'

'Then who is Mister Thomson if it is not you?'

'I have no idea.'

'Do you know Captain Ragg?'

'Yes.'

'Did you sign your name as witness to a contract of partnery between Captain Ragg and the defenders?'

'I do not remember, yea or nay. But it is possible that I did witness such a document.'

'Do you know of any relationship between any of the defenders and Captain Ragg?'

'Yes.'

'Please tell us what that relationship is.'

'Captain Ragg is cousin-german to Walter Cochran and to the spouse of Mister Fordyce.'

'Thank you. How long have you been Town Clerk?'

'Upwards of thirty years.'

'And William Fordyce and Alexander Mitchell have both been magistrates?'

'Not, I believe, since Michaelmas 1741.'

'But William Fordyce is a Justice of the Peace?'

'I believe so.'

'A Justice of the Peace or a magistrate would attest the signing of indentures?'

'Yes.'

'And you would be present?'

'I might.'

'Would you say that the magistrates took any special care to enquire of such boys as were brought before them whether they, of themselves, consented to indenting or were compelled thereto?'

'I cannot say.'

'Could any of these boys write? Or sign their names? Do you remember the contents of any of these indentures? Do you remember the terms or the dates? Do you remember witnessing any of these indentures yourself, or in fact anything to do with indentures, Mister Thomson?'

James half rose, wanting to warn Peter against losing his temper, but Peter caught his eye and, without any overt sign or wink, gave him to understand that he was enjoying the game and pretending a fervour he did not feel. Thomson also played a game. He spoke in a kind of assumed patience, as one dealing with a wilfully stupid child.

'The questions commonly put by any magistrate to an indented servant when appearing before him were, whether or not they, the indented servants, had signed their indentures willingly or if any force or compunction had been used upon them to sign, to which the indented servant gave a positive answer; and the style of the attestation on the foot of the indenture by the magistrate was that the servant compeared judicially and declared that he had willingly signed and was noways forced or compelled or enticed, and if he could not write his name it was so marked. As for the tenor of such indentures the common style of them is that servants should serve the person who signed along with him, or his assignees, in any of His Majesty's Plantations in America for a certain number of years.'

He was calm. There was no chink in this man's armour.

'These gentlemen who indent servants... Do they have any government licence or public authority or warrant to issue indentures?'

'I've already sworn that I never had any concern in this trade. I never enquired by what authority these gentlemen proceeded in their own business. I only know that, ever since I can remember, it has been the practice for ships trading from Scotland to America to indent servants for a term of years to serve there. I have often observed, in the public newspapers, advertisements for servants to indent with different merchants and ship-masters at the sea-ports. I should also like to say that I never knew of any servant being taken abroad without their indentures being attested by a magistrate and, in fact, I have often been told that indentures without such attestation are not worth a two-pence in America.'

The defenders had a last question before Thomson sat down. Hidden beneath the surface of both question and answer was a suggestion of force, but Peter could not get hold of it at this stage. When asked whether there had ever been difficulty in getting indentures issued to servants, Thomson answered that, yes, sometimes servants had run away from their masters, and he had seen complaints made to the magistrates and to the Sheriffs about it, and that he had seen warrants granted by the respective judges for apprehending and securing such runaway servants until they 'found caution to perform their indentures'.

If Thomson had given no sign of recognition of James until the mention of Cochran's wee book, James Smith, the saddler, directed everything he said towards him. He repeated his deposition in very much the same terms as he had to James that night, so many months earlier, but it was obvious that, on this occasion, he had been well prepared, since he was careful to exonerate the owners by name from any hint of kidnapping or coercion. The questioning was long and thorough. It sounded straightforward enough. He had been employed to do a job and he had done it fairly. Any attempt to throw doubt on his story met with either ignorance or denial. The shell of hard righteousness around his soft body remained intact.

'Yes, there was a boy named Peter Williamson among the number of those persons whom I engaged to go on board *The Planter*. I stationed him with Helen Law and paid her for his board and entertainment.

'Yes, I also paid Helen Law for the board of another boy called Peter Kemp, whom I had engaged in the same way.

'No I do not know whether they both went on board the ship. I did not see any of the persons I had engaged go on board. Only I heard that everyone I engaged had sailed, with the exception of one or two that deserted or were dispensed with on the application of their friends. In fact, I do not think that I was in Aberdeen when *The Planter* sailed.'

Peter got up slowly to question Smith. 'This boy, Peter Kemp, whom you engaged. Did he engage himself?'

'No. He was engaged by the consent and approbation of John Kemp, his father.'

'You have a very good memory, Mister Smith. Did the boy, Peter Williamson, engage himself?'

'I don't remember.'

'Are you sure? Would you take a good look at me, Mister Smith. It might help you to remember. Do you recognize me?'

'I cannot say for sure that you are the same Peter Williamson that I boarded with Helen Law.'

'Can you say for certain that I am not the same Peter Williamson?'

'No. And there is nothing to be gained either way. I may or I may not recognize you. Since you say you were on the ship, and since I admit that a boy named Peter Williamson was one of those I boarded with Helen Law, my recognizing you has no bearing either way. I was employed to engage servants. I employed other people as well, to board and to engage servants. I had nothing to do with either their indentures or the shipping arrangements, and I know nothing about

180

the ship or the owners of the ship. I was paid by Mister Cochran to do a job and I did it.'

'Did Walter Cochran or any of the other owners have any order or authority from the public or the government to take people into servitude?'

'I told you I know nothing about the owners. Even if they had authority from the king himself I never saw it. They were engaging servants in the very same way and manner that many other merchants in the town of Aberdeen, as well as in other places all over Scotland and in England, were practising and doing in the course of their business.'

As was proper procedure, the defenders had the last word. 'What like were conditions in those years?'

'Oh, they were poor years. Years of great dearth and scarcity. I remember that things were so bad that one woman came to me to engage her husband, which I did. The poor living in those years may have been the reason why so many people engaged to go to the Plantations.'

*

'It's not going right. We're on a road leading nowhere.' Peter was stomping up and down in the small room that George Mackie had provided with desk and chairs as well as a bed. 'Why is nobody listening?'

'They are listening. What bothers ye? Ye've two fine advocates with nothing to do except listen to ye for a whole week.'

'Oh I ken fine they're there to hear the case; but there's all the difference in the world between hearing and listening. What do they hear? They hear the ice-man, Thomson, swear blind that everything was done according to law and they hear Smith, the kidnapper himself, saying that he only did what he was told, and anyway it was only what everyone else was doing and quite lawful. I'm wasting my time here. I was better off acting to the crowds in the fairs. They listened.'

'You chose to go to law.'

Peter was taken aback for a moment. What James had said was true, but he had forgotten how he had longed for the arena of the courts after the confines of the upper room where he had first staged his drama.

'You wanted to be taken seriously. Well, look at what you've achieved. You've had Lords at your command. You've had Inner and Outer Courts give time and place to your affairs even if you were not there in person, and now, on your home ground, you've arbiters to decide penalty for those who have judged you falsely. Above all, Peter – and pay heed to this – every word these people say is written down and put on record. You may think that that's of no great matter just now, but think how afeard they were of your published word. The proceedings of the law are kept for hundreds of years and no man has the right to burn them.'

'Aye, you're right; of course you are. But how can I be sure that what is written down is the whole, bitter story? It's all so tame.'

'But that's the beauty of it. If'n you had weeping mothers and desperate men come to the court screaming for revenge, how would that read? Incoherent and unjustified rubbish, fit only for the theatre or the fairground. But here you have douce gentlemen, with quiet voices, stating in formal language that they took boys and put them in prison; that magistrates signed warrants to enslave them, and that it was done according to custom. You had them admit that they had no authority to do so, and then justify themselves by saying that everyone was doing it. Did your mother never say to you, "Two wrongs don't make a right"?'

'So you're saying I should go on?'

'I'm saying you must. Forget the flag-waving and the street corner hullabaloo! What you will have at the end of this week is a document that allows the merchants and magistrates of this and every other seaport in the land to damn themselves to perdition.'

So Peter went on.

Walter Cochran and William Fordyce produced a string of witnesses to show that, contrary to rumour, gossip or malicious slander they had been to great expense to care for the indented servants under their charge. If there were any who escaped, ran away or hid, it was because they were on to a good thing. They simply went on the loose for a day or two and re-enlisted with one of the rival shippers. Such was the frequency of this crime that the worthy merchants were forced to employ guards with whips; forced to prevent relatives from finding out where their kin were housed; forced to recapture runaways and imprison them at great inconvenience and expense.

Peter had hoped that Dod Lunen or Farquharson the Whistler, or even the fat man with the whip, Jeffrey, would have been called, but it was too much to expect. They had simply disappeared. Nobody had, seemingly, seen or heard of them from that day to this. James Robertson was called and he gently told how he was employed partly to guard, partly to ferry people, food and goods to *The Planter* as she lay at Tory. His chosen words were that he 'inspected and took care of these men, women and boys', and he was careful to point out that they were at liberty to run about and play and that he shared their accommodation and food until the ship sailed.

'Do you call to mind a boy named Williamson?'

Peter was astonished at the question. It was the resplendent figure of William Fordyce who asked it. Fordyce did not wear black, as so many of the Aberdeen merchants did, but a plum-coloured velvet coat with an embroidered waistcoat and an old-fashioned crimson sash, or baldrick, from right shoulder to left hip, as if he were accustomed to carry a sword. His lace cuffs and cravat were loose and fresh, and he stood with the weight on one leg, the other thrust forward to show his well-shaped calves.

Robertson was obviously expecting the question, as he answered without hesitation. 'To the best of my knowledge there was one of the boys, as I think called McWilliam, and this boy was a ragged, rough kind of a boy and, in my opinion, could not be under sixteen years of age. I say that because I have had boys of less stature than him, upholding the threshing of corn to me.'

'Did this McWilliam have any other name?'

'I never heard it.'

'Was there any boy called Williamson or Peter Williamson on *The Planter* when she sailed for the New World?'

'I never heard of any such. There was no other boy nor any person of the name Williamson, nor Peter Williamson on board. But on the very morning she sailed there was a number of boys who deserted and I do not remember whether, when the ship went out of the harbour into the bay and did there cast anchor, whether the boy McWilliam was amongst those remaining, who had not deserted, or not.'

Peter stood up and asked whether Robertson could identify him, on oath, as the same boy McWilliam. He did not have any hope that the answer would be anything but the elaborate denial that Robertson gave on oath. The fictional sixteen-year-old thresher of corn was so unlike Auntie Mary's scrubbed schoolboy, for all that he had been poor and no fancy dresser.

Fordyce resumed his questioning, extracting a detailed picture of the benefits of slavery. All the persons, old and young, under his charge as aforesaid, knew perfectly well where they were going, and expressed very great joy and cheerfulness at what had happened to them, as they were all well clothed and entertained – which, in the deponent's opinion, they stood in need of, as before they had but ragged clothes ... and *very* ragged! They were very well used and got a good diet – such a diet as the deponent got himself when he was overseeing them – and he heard them saying they were going to a better country than their own, and if their four years were expired or out, they would be all happy... A happy band of pilgrims!

The defenders also produced Helen Law. James had prepared Peter thoroughly for the cross-examination of Helen Law, but nothing could prepare him for the vibrant shock of her physical appearance in that dark and gloomy hall. She came, dressed in the colours of autumn, and her hair was no longer black, but henna-red. The motherly creature with two attendant swains and the hay-boxes of food that Peter recalled, or the flaunting gipsy of James' description, had been transformed into a flaming archangel of mercy. She blazed through her rehearsed statement, and then threw back her head and challenged anyone and everyone to question her. Peter smiled at her willingly, and accepted the challenge.

'Mistress Law, can you read?'

'Certainly.'

'Mister Thain, could the witness please be shown Mister Cochran's account book? Mistress Law, have you ever seen this book before?'

'I think not, but I cannot be sure.'

'Well, it's of little mind. If you look through to January 1743 you will find several references to Peter Williamson. For board of Williamson, so much, and for new shirts and for stockings, so much. Do you see that?'

'Aye, I do.'

'Thank you. Please return the book. Do you remember Peter Williamson at all?'

'I remember that there was a boy called Peter Williamson, or McWilliam, that was amongst those I brought the diet to, although he was never boarded with me.'

'Why do you remember him particularly?'

'I remember the names of most of the boys, but I can call him to mind because he spoke couthly. He was what you might style an educated boy, not rough like some of the other loons. Forbye he was poorly clad all the same and humble headed, mebbe on account of the lice. Aye, no doubt he had lice.'

'How old was this boy would you say?'

'He was a growthy lad. I'd say he was more than twelve.'

'Why do you say "more than twelve"? Why not say he was fifteen, or mebbe thirteen? What is so particular about being more than twelve?'

'I thought that was what was in dispute. Whether he was more than twelve.'

James half stood to rearrange his rug – a signal to Peter to leave well enough alone. Helen Law had gone as near to falling into the trap as it was wise to take her. She was not a stupid woman – only too helpful sometimes for her own good.

'If you take a good look at me now, Mistress Law, could you say whether I was the same Peter Williamson you remember so well?'

'No, I will not, nor I cannot, swear that you are the same.'

'But you remember a good many things about those days. Would you mind if I try to see if your remembrances are the same as mine? You had some of the girls and women boarded with you in Aberdeen? Do you remember a time when some of the big lads came to your house to see you and the girls and to have dinner with you?'

'Aye, I do. And...'

'Just a moment, Mistress Law. Let me see if I can tell the next bit. Were'nt those same boys under guard? How did they get into your house? Didn't they break down the wall?'

'So they did! And William Farquharson came and put them into the tollbooth because they had broke down the wall.'

'Did Farquharson have a fashion of breathing that was like a whistle without tune?'

'He did that! And particular when he was angry or vexed. You have him to the life there. Oh, but he was vexed at this time too with the rogues that got out. He put them into the tollbooth with the convicts. I call to mind that there was one, James Byres, that got sick when he was in the tollbooth and I speired if he could come and bide wi' me in my house till he was well, but Jeffrey said – and James Smith said alsweel – that he was no' so bad as he pretended and they'd not let me take him out until I offered to put my own son in his place. And they let me have James Byres in my house, where he stayed until he was recovered, but they let my son out of the tollbooth long before Byres was recovered out of his fever, which he was affected with for four or five days, and he had not recovered his strength, nor was he so well as before he fell sick, when he was taken back to the tollbooth or even when he was taken on board of the ship...'

Peter, seeing her pause for breath, hastily moved her on by asking her about the day that *The Planter* sailed; trying to get a different picture from the scrambled defection that had been suggested by Robertson.

'There was a treat, or entertainment, for the owners on board of Captain Ragg's ship before she sailed, to which a great many people were invited. I saw the people when I went on board to take supper to my boarders.'

'Did you know any of the people?'

'I was told by some of those on board that Baillie Fordyce and his lady were among those at the entertainment, but I do not know Baillie Fordyce or his lady. The only persons I knew, or considered to be owners, was Patrick Barron, Captain Ragg and James Smith. I know none of the other owners.'

'Thank you very much, Mistress Law.'

As ever, the defenders asked a few rounded questions of Helen Law: was she ever aware of force being used to detain servants, and so on ... repeating the same evidence over and again. Peter felt that neither of the arbiters was in any way involved in the issues of the case; they seemed to be adding up scores. One point for not acknowledging Peter, one point for swearing that no coercion was used, two points for catching runaways. Petrie would smile and nod and scratch his head, pushing his untidy wig over one ear and putting

186

it straight again with some irritation. Thain sat impassive, occasionally regarding the high polish of his shoes, occasionally calling for a break. Peter suspected that he had a supply of strong whisky in the back room of the hall, since his stillness became more somnolent, his gaze more unfocused, as the day wore on.

*

The due processes of the law took their laborious way until the time came for Peter to call his own witnesses. The small contingent of countrymen from Balnacraig and from Hirnley were welcomed and shaken by the hand as they stamped the cold from their feet and placed folded wraps and bonnets at the side of the hall. Peter felt a tightness in his throat at these honest fellows, led by Francis Fraser of Findrack and John Wilson of Cloak, who had come into the town on his behalf. They soon let him know, however, that there was nothing but pride in what they were doing, and that they would have gone to the capital itself, if necessary, to do their duty by Peter's father that was their neighbour.

What Peter had not expected, nor James either, was that the defenders would get up and leave. Fordyce simply walked from the room, but Walter Cochran took the trouble to offer a small bow to the arbiters and another mocking obeisance to Peter before turning smartly on the raised heels of his little shoes and leaving the hall.

'Can they do that?' Peter whispered to James.

'They're not on trial. This is an arbitration and I suppose they're under no obligation to stay. The arbiters do not seem in the least surprised, so I take it they knew that they planned to leave at this point.'

'But I thought they'd want to question my evidence. Don't they want to examine any of the witnesses?'

'Presumably not. It is byway of a deep insult, if you look at it. It's like they're saying that they don't care what you adduce in evidence; they've had their say and now let the arbiters arbitrate.'

'But I must go on.'

'Of a surety you must. These good people have come a long way to tell the truth, and the arbiters must be given every opportunity to hear them. But be careful, Peter. For the very reason that the defenders scorn your evidence, you must be sure that you deliver it strong, but without embroidery. No-one must be able to say that your witnesses were unreliable.'

'Are you ready, Mr Williamson?' Petrie was scratching and irritable.

'Certainly, sir. Without interruption from the defenders this will not take long.'

'We're glad to hear it. Please proceed.'

Peter felt strong and well. The absence of antipathy warmed him and he took James' warning to heart. The biblical figure of John Wilson of Cloak stood majestic and incapable of untruth and would surely have held rock firm, even had there been any questioning. Peter let him say his piece and thanked him gravely. He held the reins tight on the volatile Fraser, and encouraged Peter Cromar of Burnside over his nervousness to tell again of the search James Williamson had made for his captured son. Peter turned to the arbiters...

'You have already seen the certificate of baptism and the record of my schooling that shows that I was a child of less than twelve when I was taken and barely twelve years old when I was shipped into slavery. You have the sworn statement of William Wilson, one of the crew of *The Planter*, who very well remembers me and who testifies to the barbarous treatment all the servants received upon the occasion of the wreck, when we were abandoned to our fate, women and children alike, the brave captain and crew taking the only longboat and saving themselves first. This I trust you have read and appreciated. Many people have given evidence on oath, and this evidence has been presented before their lordships in Edinburgh, that tells the truth of the whole trade of these merchant kidnappers. Aye, I know it is not the business of this hearing to question what rightly belongs to other folk and not only to me, but it is the truth and no slander. It was what was in my book that caused the magistrates to burn it in fear. It has not been possible to bring the men who laid hands on me, as on other boys and girls and kept them shut away from rescue until the time came to spirit them on board ship. The names I had for them may not have been their real names, and they are unlikely to come forward to answer for their crimes.'

'Their alleged crimes.'

'Aye, to be sure ... their *alleged* crimes. But I should, nevertheless,

188

wish you to look at what the other witnesses say about those men, as well as those who worked for Bonny John. And now I would like to examine the defenders, Walter Cochran and William Fordyce.'

'Ah ... no.' Petrie looked at Thain who, without returning his look, shook his head. 'They have made their statements, as you have, before the Court of Sessions and here. They have also produced witnesses and allowed you to question those witnesses.'

'But I must be allowed to question them!'

'This is not a court of criminal justice, Mister Williamson. There is no "must" about it. We are here to arbitrate between you and the merchants of Aberdeen. The other party, having presented their material, ask us to delay no longer but come speedily to a decision, and have now left about their business. If you have done then you must leave as well and we will let you know our decreet-arbitral in due course.'

'But...'

'No, Mister Williamson. There is no more to be said. Mister Maclaurin, you are a man of the law, if not a qualified lawyer. Please explain to "Indian Peter" that this is correct procedure and tell him that he must abide by it. And now, good day to you both.'

Chapter 26

The greatest advantage of going to arbitration is the speed with which decisions can be obtained. The hearing ended on November the eleventh and the very next day the arbiters announced that they could not agree.

Both arbiters agreed that damages were due to Peter. They agreed with the law lords (how could they do less?) that he had been wrongfully arrested, shamefully used and deprived of a variety of liberties to which any free man was entitled, and they agreed, having heard the latest evidence, that Peter had been telling the truth. But they disagreed fundamentally on the amount of the damages. Thain thought five hundred pounds, Petrie thought one tenth of that amount. Such a vast difference, in principle as well as in fact, caused them to say that they would take the matter to the oversman, Charles Forbes of Shiels, Sheriff-substitute.

The final date for a decree was the fifteenth of November, which was Monday. They all well knew that if no decision had been reached by that time the whole case would be declared void and referred back to the courts in Edinburgh.

James regarded it as significant that none of the defenders was in the hall to hear the decreet. They had relied on Petrie, their 'doer', and continued to scorn the proceedings. The old law clerk was not surprised at what had come about. He was too wise in the ways of men to be hurt by their indifference and the suggestion of collusion between the defenders and their representative, nor was he particularly concerned to alter the situation. To his mind there was much to be said in having the whole affair back in the hands of the Edinburgh courts. There things were orderly, if slow, and Andrew could take his rightful place again before the lords of justice. But first they must seem to be abiding by the decision to bring in the oversman. He went forward to talk to Thain about having vital pieces of evidence placed before Charles Forbes, and only then did he notice that Peter had gone.

Knowing Peter's tempestuous impatience with the law, he imagined him taking to the wild hills as he had done before, walking and wounding himself into self-respect again. We can manage without him, he thought. Cochran and Fordyce leave it to their advocates; let's see how we get on.

James had got it wrong. Peter had not taken to the hills. Maclaurin had often described him to others as a survivor, as a man who had suffered so much that he had learnt to bear injury without complaint. What he did not understand, however, was that, having begun to fight back, Peter had now ceased to bear injury as a humble victim and had become vulnerable again. He had re-lived the old wounds and healed them, but he was as susceptible as any man to the hurt of injustice and rejection. Black anger had threatened to drown him, but it was a force he could use. He left the church hall on the crest of the wave and stormed off to find Forbes.

At first he went blindly, without thinking, but then made for Mackie's to tap into the network of information his hostelry represented.

'Where'll I find the Sheriff-substitute?'

'You've tried the Sheriff Court, no doubt?'

'No. I'll go there, but it'll not serve if the court is in session. He's to oversee my case and he's not been near. The two idiot advocates cannot agree and the sand is running out. We have to get him to re-hear the depositions all over again. We only have today and tomorrow and then it's Sunday. Monday will be too late. Monday is the day the decreet-arbitral must be announced. George, help me. What can I do?'

'If he's in court, bring him here to eat. They must recess for midday dinner. You, above all people, should know that, Peter.'

'Aye, that's good sense, as always, George. I'll bespeak a table from you. Does he drink?'

'Like a fish. I'll lay on the best and plenty. Now go and find him.'

'I'll bring him here if'n I have to drag him.'

He found Forbes, but he was not in court. The Sheriff-substitute's conception of being an oversman was plainly one of being on call.

Maybe someone knew how to find him, but it was by dint of tracing him step by step from the Sheriff's door that Peter heard he would be 'busy with a hot punch at Bains' – and so he was. It was now well past eleven in the morning and the man was obviously in no fit state to be taken far. Mackie's was quite out of the question and the imperious drunkard sent Peter scurrying to the New Inn to bespeak him dinner.

Peter did not take long. Nevertheless, when he came back, Forbes had disappeared.

From this point on, as so often in the affairs of men, the serious drama became a deadly farce, which Peter played with the fury and energy of his anger. He was told that Forbes' 'Great Companion, Collector Finlayson', had trepanned Forbes of Shiels and spirited him away. It transpired that Finlayson was a man 'much engaged with the defenders', and Peter feared the worst. Forbes was a juicy bone and the dogs were out.

Like all good farce, the scenery contains a number of doors and it was behind one such door that Peter found the Sheriff-substitute with his great companion.

'I've taken a table at the New Inn, sir. Will you dine now?' Peter adopted the role of servitor, which he had perfected over many years, from waiting on lawyers. 'Everything you ordered is ready and like to spoil, if'n you do not come at once, sir.'

He could not avoid a snub to Finlayson, but was sure that he must get some solid food into Forbes before asking him to attend to the matter of his arbitration.

They made a surprisingly steady and dignified progress to dinner and the Sheriff-substitute laid down a good foundation of pastry, meat and pudding. Peter hovered, acting both as host and fellow diner. It was not surprising that eating in a common dining-room which had been bespoken by Forbes himself, they should be pounced on by all his acquaintance. There was nothing Peter could do or say to prevent Forbes entertaining his friends and colleagues. The man sat, like a tribal chief, dispensing largesse in the form of greetings, drinks, invitations to join their table, and plans for spending the rest of the day, and night, in carousal. Peter's attempts at introducing 'arbitration' into the proceedings sounded like the bleating of some billy-kid protesting against slaughter. He was relieved beyond measure when he

192

saw, coming into the room, purposefully and armed with tied bundles of papers, a defending force to break the siege.

'James, thank God you've come. Yon's our oversman! Will Thain bring him round, do you think?'

Thain put the papers on an empty chair and anchored them with his cloak and hat, neatly spread.

'Charles, we need your help. We need a decision on this matter by Monday morning. I've all the papers here for you, and I see Mister Williamson has already primed you as to the situation...' Peter shook his head vigorously. 'No? Oh well, it'll not take you long. It's plain that the man should get compensation for the wrongs done him in the past. Petrie and I only disagree on the amount.'

'Should he not consider the whole evidence?'

'Not necessary, Mister Williamson, not at all necessary.' Thain took out a lace-edged kerchief and flicked away some errant crumbs that offended him. 'There's no need for any more than a plain choice of whether I am right in asking for the proper sum of five hundred pounds, to be paid by the persons concerned and not from public funds, or whether Petrie's paltry fifty is nearer the mark. I'm sure you would like the Sherrif-substitute to think about that, Mister Williamson.'

'But, would he not be better able to decide if he heard the whole story?'

'No time, Peter,' interrupted James. 'Let the situation remain simple, or let time run out and I'll take it back to Andrew.'

'Stuff and nonsense!' Forbes spluttered more crumbs onto the cloth. 'Do you think I'm incapable of arbitrating between the lot of ye? I'll take all the papers away with me and I'll give you a reasoned judgement before Monday. Have you signed your disagreement, you and Petrie?'

'I will do it now, sir.'

'Aye do, and get the other fellow to sign too. Call yourselves advocates? I'll show you how an arbitration should be done. A matter of simple decision-making. You'll never get on in this business, John Thain, if you cannot make decisions unafraid. I'll take the papers and let you know later. Now go! You're spoiling my dinner!'

The dapper advocate took up his cloak and hat and ostentatiously nudged the papers into James' care before leaving. It was surely never a wink that he gave James in parting – it was more of a discreet lowering of the eyelid – but he seemed totally unabashed by the Sheriff-substitute's growling. James took charge of the papers, following Thain's example and bundling them in his cloak. There was little or no chance that Forbes would look at them that day, however. The dinner turned into a party and the party into a rout and the rout into a riot, before ever James took himself and the papers off to the comparative sobriety of George Mackie's establishment.

Forbes' capacity for drink was unbelievable. They stayed, close drinking, helter-skelter, until the clock struck eleven, when Charles Forbes slid, without warning, sideways off his chair and lay snoring on the floor. The landlord was insistent.

'You canna leave him sackless on the flair, man. Get him awa', out o' here and intae's ain chaumer. I'll lend ye a couple o' ma' lassies to guide ye. It's no far.'

The lassies were delighted and made great fun of the burdensome Sheriff, removing his breeches to his knees, painting his face with rouge, and placing his fluffy, great wig over his male nakedness. They got hold of a handcart from somewhere and between them – the two sober, but giggling girls and the less than sober Williamson – trundled him off to bed.

'You'd best not be here when he wakes, the morn. Come home with us and we'll look after ye.'

Peter declined their offer as courteously as he could. There was a nagging voice in his head that rang the timer: Monday morning is too late ... tomorrow we'll be sober... He had to get back to James while there was still some night left. He allowed the two sisters, for that is what they were, to ride him back to the New Inn on the cart and then, kissing them warmly and giving them a shilling each, he took himself home to Mackie's.

George purged him and washed him out and fed him again, in an attempt to clear the alcohol from his brain. Peter was reasonably clear-headed when he woke around eleven the next morning, although he still had a headache. He breakfasted gingerly on a concoction of lemon, raw eggs and brandy, which George swore would set him up for the day. James, who had already been up and about for some time, sat and listened while Peter told him about taking Forbes home.

'I doubt he'll stir a foot outside the house today. He said he would

194

take the papers and shut himself up with them, so we'd best fetch everything round to his house and make sure that the others don't get to him first.'

'You don't think that mebbe they've already done just that?'

'Got to him? He was dead to the world! The way we placed him, the girls and I, if'n anyone catches glimpse of him, he'd never dare show his face in public again! I doubt he'll open the door to anyone, but we'll be sure he gets these depositions, even if we have to sit by him while he reads them.'

'Aye, we'll do that, but I'm still afeared. There's a power about these men when they get together. I have no doubt at all that Fordyce and Cochran got Petrie, if not Thain as well, to disagree so widely on purpose, in order to force them to bring in the oversman. We know that they two defenders and Captain Ragg are all of the same family, as it were, and that the merchants and magistrates are closely involved in the whole business. Now Forbes is one of them. He's probably shared a courtroom with Baillie Fordyce, and, from what you tell me, he's a venal man and a drunkard. He'll have been got at, before ever you came to arbitration.'

'All the more reason to get him in our grasp. With Cochran's wee book before him and the depositions from the Court of Sessions itself ... what ails you?'

'Thain didna' give me the wee book!'

'Are you sure?'

'Aye, while you were "attending" to the Sheriff-substitute last night, I sorted all the papers and did them up in oilskin against the salt air. The book wasnae there.'

'Where'll it be?'

'Thain will have it in his pocket, no doubt. I'd best seek him out and get him to bring it to Forbes.'

'Aye, for without the evidence of their complicity Fordyce and Cochran could simply say I'm lying. For God's sake, James, get the wee book, or I'm sunk!'

The two men went their separate ways, James to the advocate's rooms and Peter to the house of Forbes of Shiels.

*

195

The derelict, rusting bell-pull eventually produced a derelict, rusting housekeeper. Peter was not surprised that she had not appeared last night; he wondered that she could make it thus far to answer the door. He guessed she must be some elderly relative, and when she gave him the conventional answer to his query – 'Shiels is not at home' – he pushed her aside and swept up the stairs. True enough, Forbes was not in his bed. He was not in the closet, nor under the bed, nor was he in any of the rooms in the large old house.

'I swear he'll no' have gone by his own legs. What have you done with him, woman?'

'And what's that to you, Mister?'

'I represent a law partnership from Edinburgh, and I'm here about the business of the law. It's important that I find your... The Sheriff-substitute ... at once – for his own sake as well as my own. You'd best tell me where he is.'

'I dinna ken whaur he is. Mister Forbes was in no state to stir from his bed, when one comes jingling and jangling, like yourself, and hauls him off and conveys him away.'

'And at what o'clock was that, Mistress?'

'Before nine. Boggie had him dressed, for the puir man was in no fashion to be seen, and into a carriage as the clock struck nine.'

'Who, or what, is Boggie?'

'Frae Edinburgh, ye say? Aye, 'twill be so, and you no' tellin' William Boggie that's clerk to the Collector.'

'Collector Finlayson?'

'Aye, he's the one.'

'And you do not know where they went?'

'I do not.'

'Well, I think I know. My thanks to you, Mistress.' And Peter fairly ran away from the house, and into the street towards Bains.

Forbes was not at Bains. He was not at the New Inn, nor at any of the intervening places of public resort. At last Peter went to Thain's rooms and there found James had left him a message to say that he was taking dinner with the arbiters at Jimmy Hay's. He came over to where they were sitting around a corner table in noisy good humour. Once more Peter felt the black shadow of resentment at his exclusion from their world rise up in him like the bile of last night's excesses.

They welcomed him over and ordered a meal that he was not able to enjoy. They assured him that the papers and the wee book had been given to Forbes and that the messenger had returned with the information that the Sheriff-substitute had promised to shut himself up with the papers until three o'clock, when he would see both parties. Meanwhile they were passing the time in swapping stories of past cases, each one wrapped in a high degree of legal jargon: in praesenti ... in gremio legis ... in fieri ... in flagrante delicto ... in extremis ... in loco parentis ... in media res. It all seemed like childish time-wasting to Peter, who had no Latin and who cared little for such showing off.

'Is it not time we went to see the Sheriff-substitute?' Peter asked for the third time, as childish as the others in his impatience and ill temper. 'Where is he? I'll go and get Cochran and Fordyce to come where he is.'

'Oh, they'll not come. We're to represent them.'

'Well, shall we not go? Tell me where to find Forbes and I'll go myself.'

'He's at home. I gather he has still all the marks upon him of a man not half slept out his last debauch.'

'Quondam se bene gesseret...' James could not resist a final dig.

'He's not at home!' Peter bellowed. 'I've been there and hunted through the house. He was fetched to that bosom companion of his, Collector Finlayson, but I have no idea where.'

'On your feet, gentlemen!' James was authoritative. 'We'll go to his house at once, in case he's returned there. It's nigh on three.'

'I'll go to look for your messenger. If he still has the papers and if he's been lying I will not come to you to defend me on a charge of wilful murder, you can be sure of that. What's his name and where'll I find him?'

'Alex Mitchell.'

'What? You gave our papers to Alexander Mitchell? James, did you know? Alexander Mitchell! Why he's in it with them. His is one of the names on the list of owners. Baillie Mitchell! And you gave him our papers. God Almighty! He was only kept out of the charge because, along with Barron, he seemed to have nothing to do with indenting servants ... but to give him our papers... Where'll I find him?'

197

Thain and Petrie exchanged worried looks. Then Petrie, shrugging on his coat ready to go out, said, 'He's a good man, Baillie Mitchell. I'll swear to it. He'll maybe come to his brother's tavern. You could look there.'

'Peter, don't spoil the ship now for a ha'porth of tar. Don't let them put you in the wrong at this end of the day. There's more than just you depending on this case, remember. Go gently!'

'Aye, I'll go gentle as a maid with a kitten, but I'll kill the man if he's betrayed us, so help me God.'

It was then well into the afternoon. Peter enquired for directions to find Robert Mitchell's tavern. To save time he also went in to every tavern, drinking or eating shop, and every evil howff by the way, asking for Forbes and Collector Finlayson. At one elevated establishment by the name of Campbell's, the serving men and maids denied the presence of either gentlemen as they carried supplies of porter, white wine and punch into the back room. Peter, for some reason, was certain that they were lying and tried to force his way in. Campbell himself employed a strong door-man and Peter's demands to be allowed to look into the chamber were, at a signal from the landlord, cut short by a severe blow on the back of his head. Peter eventually found himself lying on the pavement, dazed, sickened, and even more angry. As he worked his way to his feet by holding on to the pole that supported the furze bush that was the inn sign, he thought he heard the raucous sound of a drinking song:

> Now let us all agree
> Arbiter shall arbitrate,
> But to help his concentration
> Put another one on the slate;
> And here's to you, For-biss.
> Here's to you, my jolly soul,
> And with you we'll take a draught
> Before we go to bed.
> Here's to you, For-biss.
> Here's to you, For-biss.

Maybe it was the blow on the head causing the singing noise; anyway, there was no chance of getting into the tavern again. Several well-mannered citizens, their wives and children, crossed over the street as Peter lurched from embracing the post to stagger on towards Mitchell's place. He felt the back of his head and saw blood on his fingers, but it would dry. He had received worse than that, and in some strange way it was familiar, almost a comfort, to be again in a world where you staggered on, wounded and bleeding, to meet your enemy face to face, swords drawn. He had no weapon but his anger, yet he felt assured of the battle to come.

As he opened the door of Mitchell's tavern he saw them all – Cochran, Fordyce, Barron and Alex Mitchell – and they saw him, bleeding, dirty and as pale as a ghost.

'Here's the paleface!'

'No warpaint, Delaware?'

'Get some pinions and some pitch and we'll tar and feather ye.'

Peter took a firm grip on the back of a chair and drew himself up. 'Alexander Mitchell, where's the papers you were to take to the Sheriff-substitute?'

'With the Sheriff-substitute.'

'Oh aye, and where'll he be at this moment?'

'No doubt signing the arbitration.'

'I said "where?"'

'Why, where else would he be but in his own house?'

'Perhaps at Campbells?'

Peter wanted to say more. He wanted to find out how much they knew, how far they were playing him along like a hungry trout, but the room was advancing and retreating from him and there was a hissing and singing in his ears that made it difficult to think. The men at the table seemed to be shouting.

'Why would he be there?'

'But'n if he were, what's the harm in that?'

'You need no courthouse to make a decrees arbitral.'

'All along you've deliberately tried to delay things, Williamson. You are obsessed with your own righteousness.'

'This so-called "kidnapping book" is no more than an ordinary account book.'

'Yon ship's book too – what's so pertinent about that?'

199

'You're accusing us of crimes. Where does it say that indented servants are slaves? Where does it say that taking servants from a life of poverty is a crime?'

'You're living in the kingdom of the mooncalves, Indian! The New World's turned your head. They're a seditious bunch over there, they say.'

'What's America to us?'

'What's your fantasy fiction of Indians and slavery to the Sheriff-substitute?'

'He needs no papers to come to the right decision, paleface. He's only to say fifty pounds instead of five hundred.'

Peter felt his knees weak and his head spinning. He turned the chair and sat heavily astride it, leaning forward over the back.

'You may be very cock-a-whoop now, gentlemen, but I tell you that you have not finished with me yet.'

'Williamson, are you using threats towards us?'

'Yes, I am, and if you like to call over some of your cronies here, I'll threaten you before witnesses. If I find that Forbes has not been given all the evidence; if I find that any or all of you gentlemen, with Petrie and Thain, have got together on this matter and are preventing me from seeing the arbiter; I PROTEST ... I will...'

Peter fell forward. Only the back of the chair connecting with the edge of the table saved him from crashing to the ground.

*

It was seven o'clock that evening before Peter came to, in his bed at George Mackie's.

'How'd I get here?'

'You've friends as well as enemies, my son.' James was holding a damp cloth to his head. It was cool and he felt no desire to move away from the cool calm of the old man's tenderness. 'They carried you all the way home. Man, you gave us a fright! I thought you were dead.'

'Cochran and the others ... they're all in this together...'

'I know. They told me what went on at Mitchells. There were folks there that saw you, and heard what was said. They told me you were like a spirit come from hell to haunt your enemies. But they

200

couldna' say how you came by the blood on your face and head. It's a fair dunt, Peter. Who gave it ye?'

'Some fella in the place where Forbes is holed up. They hit me from behind and threw me out. Probably hit me again.'

'You said you'd go gentle!'

'He was there. I swear he was there. But I could not come at him. There's too much against us father.'

'Whisht now. Lie down and be quiet. There's naught to do until Monday. Take the Sabbath to rest and mend your head.'

'With vinegar and brown paper.'

Peter smiled weakly, and whether he faded into unconsciousness again or whether he was just too weak to keep his eyes open James could not be sure. George Mackie came in with fresh water, cold from the well and, backed by a crowd of anxious faces at the door, enquired after Peter's state.

'He knows me. He is clear about what happened. He's a survivor, my boy; he'll do well.'

'Aye? Is that so? That's fine now.'

There was even some faint applause from the folk at the door before they were shut out and George and James took turn by turn to watch over Indian Peter's bed until morning.

*

When Peter opened his eyes the next morning it was to the sound of bells.

It was Sunday morning and he had woken to the weak sun of a windy and damp daylight with the promise of more rain, and all the bells in town ringing the faithful to worship. Peter stretched and turned and felt none the worse, until he tried to sit up, when knives and needles of pain ran through his head and neck. He closed his eyes and lay back. It was Sunday, and there was nothing he could do to further his cause on a Sunday.

After a while George came in with one of the maids and a basin of warm water to wash his head. They had not wanted to touch it the previous evening but now it was time to cut his hair and see the extent of the damage. The cut itself was small, the skin broken only in a small area, but obviously, as George pointed out with great glee,

201

the doorman at Campbells knew how to give him a headache: the whole of the back of his skull was tender and bruised and he was lucky that it was not smashed in like a boiled egg.

'Where's James?' said Peter, when the girl had gone off to empty the basin. 'Has he gone to the kirk?'

'Na, na. He's away to pay a Sunday goodwill call on the Sheriff-substitute – just to enquire how the poor man does, ye ken. He'll be back before long.'

Peter was not sure whether he ought to be worried at this piece of news, but as the maid came in at this moment with porridge and bannocks and warm milk for the invalid, and because she was a bonny lass and kind, and because he had eaten nothing to speak of the previous day, he decided he was hungry and that James was old enough to look after himself.

The food warmed and settled him and he slept again. When he woke next, James was there, packing his clothes into a bag.

'How was the Sheriff-substitute?'

'Fou' and sackless as a bairn. He'll keep his bed till morn.'

'Will that be time to make his decreet? Tomorrow morning?'

James came over and sat beside Peter. He looked him close in the face and said, 'Son, ye'll have to move. So soon as ye're fit ye'll have to be away from here.'

'Why? What's afoot?'

'All the time you were looking for them, those douce baillies and merchants had the Sheriff-substitute penned up at Campbells. They fed him white wine, punch, cooling draughts of porter, and a large dose of spirits in quick succession, and he signed the arbitration at one o'clock yesterday.'

'But they were in Robert Mitchell's place. I saw them there!'

'The general does not need to be on the field of battle. He can send in the infantry to do the fighting for him. Collector Finlayson had a two-three men with him: one was his own clerk, William Boggie, another was David Morice who is Deputy Sheriff Clerk. Morice has copies of the decree. He was reading it to his acquaintance, and to the world at large, this morning as they went to church.'

'And I take it that this decree goes against us?'

'Aye, and it goes far beyond the plain facts of whether it is fifty or

202

five hundred pounds. He assoilzies Walter Cochran, William Fordyce, Alexander Mitchell and Patrick Barron altogether. I'm sorry Peter.'

'So I am the guilty one?'

'Aye and still subject to their previous sentence of banishment.'

'And there is no truth in us.'

'And there is no truth in us.'

Peter turned away his head. Two hot tears of weakness oozed from his closed eyes and lay on his lashes. He was too weak, too empty, to feel anger or resentment.

'Let's go home, fayther, shall we?'

Chapter 29

They did not leave that day. There was no-one to take them and James was loth to put Peter, in his weakness, through such a long journey. Although it had been the old clerk who had first wanted to pack and go, on reflection he wanted to do things the right way, so that when his other boy, his Andrew, asked him for a true account he could claim absolute correctitude within the law. So he went to the advocate's rooms on the last day of the allotted time, collected a copy of the decree and gave thanks to Thain for his advocacy on their behalf, all as if he knew nothing of any malpractice. The advocate bowed him out, apologizing for the failure of the suit.

'The oversman maturely and deliberately considered the depositions and has made out the decreet-arbitral in full, and I am only sorry that it went against us. I believe Mister Williamson did not help his cause by attempting to delay affairs with talk of material not being available. But, you know, the so-called kidnapping book was in my pocket the whole time I was with Forbes. It was not submitted because any material evidence was inserted in the documents from Edinburgh. As for the ship's papers, Mister Maclaurin, there was nothing pertinent in that document, as you are probably well aware.'

'So all is well?'

'Aye, all is well, except that I am sorry that your man was put to all this pother over something which perhaps would have been best left alone. He is in good health, I trust?'

'He is in some little distress, I have to say, and this will not help his spirits to mend. But that is the way of things in this world, is it not?'

'You'll be returning straight away?'

'There's no reason why we should stay longer, is there?'

'None at all, none at all.'

James sat a long time on the cold stone base of the Mercat Cross reading through the decreet-arbitral. There were three pages. Although this was a copy, at the bottom of each page was a statement that it had been signed by Charles Forbes of Shiels, Sheriff-substitute. The words were unequivocal and harsh. After a long preamble about Thain and Petrie it went on: 'Having heard the parties and their agents fully anent the matters in dispute and having a good conscience before my eyes I give forth and pronounce my decreet-arbitral and final sentence in the matters submitted, to wit, I find that the said Peter Williamson hath not proven that the kidnapping or illegally seducing or transporting to America boys or others was practised or carried on by the saids Walter Cochran, William Fordyce, Alexander Mitchell and Patrick Barron or any other by their order: And that he hath not proven that he himself was kidnapped or illegally seduced and transported by the saids Walter Cochran ... and therefore I assoilzie from the summons and process intended the said Walter Cochran, William Fordyce, Alexander Mitchell, and Patrick Barron...'

He folded the documents slowly and became aware there was a small, silent group looking down at him.

'You'll be away then.'

It was not a question but a resignation.

'So it seems.

'Now you see how things are.'

'Aye, now I see.'

'An' yon Indian Peter. He'll no be dancin' in the streets just now?'

'No, Mistress. There'd be little to gain from all that.'

'But they were dancing, dancing and jubi-latin'. At the very doors o' the kirk they were dancing.'

It was Mistress Brown who spoke. James looked more closely and saw, with a shock of disbelief, that these were the people of Aberdeen who had first sought the old clerk out to give evidence against their own masters. A tall sailor stepped forward, canvas bag on his shoulder. It was Peter Kemp.

'My ship sails in an hour. If you want passage out of this place I can take you on board. It's not the end of the world. There's green trees and the wind blowing in other places too. They're not evil men at heart, you know; only they have been given power over the lives of others and that is the one thing they care about – keeping hold of their own poor ounce or two of power. Come now, or we'll miss the tide, and that's a force you cannot ignore.'

James tucked the papers in his breast and stood up briskly. The other men and women touched his arm, or took his hand, or patted his shoulder in shared acceptance of fate and left him to go with Stookie.

Peter was up when they got back to the inn and, with one of George's blankets about his shoulder, the two men half carried him onto the ship. The people were there on the quay. Now there was a crowd. They pressed about Peter, thanking him for trying, giving him food and their blessing, promising him that one day...

'Give us a wee one o' they songs, Peter.'

'Something of a farewell, eh?'

'No, that'll not do at all!'

Peter let the blanket fall to one side so that it hung, Indian fashion over one shoulder. Hair streaming about his bruised scalp he raised an arm to the sky and, standing above them on the plank, he tipped his head back and in a high voice he sang the eagles down from the sky. It was a war chant, and as he thudded one heel relentlessly down on the plank, others joined in the rhythm – down, down, down – beating on the stones and thudding against the sides of the old ship until the bo'sun's whistle cut through the alien sound and men ran forward to cast off and raise the gangplank.

Epilogue

It might have ended there, but the world is not like that. When the Crosbies heard what had happened they pounced upon a small loophole in the arbitration, and the law lords finally overturned the arbiter's decree on the grounds that it had been read out on the Sabbath. Thus, by a technicality, as is the way of the law, Peter Williamson, who brought a case against slavery and kidnapping, finally won. It is important to remember that this was on the third of December, in the year seventeen hundred and sixty-eight – some fifty years before Wilberforce obtained the abolition of slavery in Britain, and almost one hundred years before Abraham Lincoln and the American Civil War.

There is a legend that by the time the final turn in the legal history of Indian Peter came to pass, and Baillie William Fordyce was dead and buried, that his coffin was opened and found to be full of stones. Like some of the other detail in the story it may not be true. Peter Williamson was, however, very real. He used his restless energy to establish a directory of Edinburgh and to establish the penny post in that city. His coffee shop is celebrated in *The Rising of the Session* by Robert Ferguson:

> This vacance is a heavy doom
> On Indian Peter's coffee-room,
> For, a' his china pigs are toom;
> Nor do we see
> In wine the sucker biscuits soom
> As light's a flee.

Williamson's books, which are little more than pamphlets, survive, and the court cases in all their complexity of claim and counter claim are preserved in eighteenth-century print in the Advocates' Library in Edinburgh.

From these and other sources this story has been put together. There are moments when the information runs out, but these are few and far between. For the most part, this is the true history of Indian Peter.